DEADLY
SAN DIEGO

DEADLY
SAN DIEGO

HISTORIC HOMICIDES AND COLD CASES

STEVE WILLARD

THE
History
PRESS

Published by The History Press
Charleston, SC
www.historypress.com

Cover images courtesy of the San Diego Police Museum.

First published 2022

Manufactured in the United States

ISBN 9781467152792

Library of Congress Control Number: 2022939428

Notice: The information in this book is true and complete to the best of our knowledge. It is offered without guarantee on the part of the author or The History Press. The author and The History Press disclaim all liability in connection with the use of this book.

For Julie E.M. Willard

CONTENTS

ACKNOWLEDGEMENTS

The challenges of writing about crimes that occurred almost one hundred years ago are monumental. It's only through the assistance of the following people and the vast archives of the San Diego Police Museum that this project ever saw the light of day. As such, thanks are extended to the following people:

Ed Stotler, for direct information on his father, Officer Thomas Edwin "Ed" Stotler.

From the San Diego Police Department, Detective Sergeant Jim Arthur (retired), Detective Rick Carlson (retired), Criminalist Tess Hemmerling and Detective Sergeant Tony Johnson (retired).

For assistance with the forensics, I thank Senior Latent Print Examiner Laurie Becker Torres (Chula Vista Police Department, retired).

For re-creating a very detailed rendering of the French family home, the assistance of Viet Do was immeasurable.

Special thanks to retired San Diego Police Lieutenant Tom Giaquinto. Without his obsessive diligence toward the untold stories of Officer Herbert Webster and Detective Charles Harris, the tragic story of both men would have been forever lost to time.

Special thanks is also in order to San Diego Police Sergeant Patrick Vinson (retired). His ability to connect obscure events, locations and individuals brought the John Latham story to life.

Lastly, if not for exceptional detail toward investigations and twenty years of case notes from the late Detective Lieutenant Ed Dieckmann, this project simply could not have been completed.

INTRODUCTION

A 1925 *Los Angeles Times Sunday Magazine* cover story by John Steven McGroarty opined, "It is a strange thing, indeed, that the world has been so slow to find its way to San Diego. It has always been a wonder to us—this strange thing. A spot so surpassingly alluring in its beauty, so glamorous with romance, and that was ever so potential in its commercial position of strategic mastery. But, the world has a way of learning at last. And now it is making a pathway to San Diego's door—to its puerta del sol, the doorway of the sun.…The vision of San Diego taking her place among the great cities of the earth is so clear and vivid now that even the dullest mind cannot fail to see it."

Despite the glowing review, history has hidden a dark, sinister underbelly of the sprawling metropolis now known as "America's Finest City," a catchphrase coined by the Mayor at the time, Pete Wilson, in 1972.

Among the darkest stories are the rampant violent crime in the crown jewel of the city, Balboa Park, and the unsolved slayings of two police officers.

There also exists the possibility that a phantom sex slayer terrorized San Diego in the decade prior to World War II.

In a small, tight-knit community, mere speculation that a homicidal bogeyman was lurking in the shadows, just waiting to slaughter his or her next innocent victim, launched an unprecedented municipal frenzy of fear.

The media didn't help. As late as 1947, some outlets attempted to connect the slaying of the Black Dahlia to the mysterious San Diego sex slayer.

1

A LONG, PAINFUL DEMISE

MAY 1924.

Thirty-eight-year-old Officer Herbert T. Webster Sr. was assigned to uniformed patrol duties out of the Ocean Beach substation seven miles north and west of the Downtown Police Headquarters.

At that time, Ocean Beach was a relatively isolated, sleepy beachfront hamlet with stunning views and little crime.

A native of Michigan, Webster was a nine-year veteran of the San Diego Police Department (SDPD) and came to the city in 1915. He had worked the Ocean Beach District all but three months of his SDPD career.

The Webster family was so committed to the community that they made Ocean Beach their home and resided in a modest residence at 1919 Cable Street.

A veteran of the Great War (later known as World War I) who left the ranks of the SDPD to serve overseas, Webster is seen in photos as a fair-haired policeman who wore his olive-drab, wool uniform confidently. His department-issued silver badge, number 22, a shield with a five-point star cut into the center, was worn on the left side of his chest covering his heart.

Like the majority of the uniformed force, Officer Webster carried a six-shot revolver and a set of steel handcuffs under his thigh-length tunic. A heavy lead sap, shrouded in black cowhide, hung from a secondary pocket sewn into the back side of one leg of his trousers.

Sergeant George Churchman on the front porch of the Ocean Beach substation around 1925. Located at 1922 Abbott Street, the small substation was moved across the street to a larger facility at 1951 Abbott in 1927. That building still exists and is home to a retail store. *Courtesy of San Diego Police Museum.*

As with many early twentieth-century law enforcement agencies, police vehicular mechanization was still in its relative infancy, and the one-hundred-member San Diego Police Department did not maintain a marked fleet of prowl cars.

To address the need to patrol areas outside the downtown core, the department paid a twenty-five-dollar monthly stipend to specific officers to drive their own vehicles for patrol duty. The cars were not marked with what would now be a traditional paint scheme or with police designation.

The advent of a two-way police radio by which an officer could immediately request assistance didn't come to San Diego until 1935. To compensate, the SDPD used a variety of ways for officers to receive calls.

Each patrolman assigned to a beat was required to check in at one of the many police callboxes across the city every thirty minutes. The phone number for officers was MAin1202.

For more pressing needs, a crew of Emergency Riders sat astride their Harley Davidson or Indian motorcycles in an alley adjacent to headquarters.

For urgent calls that could not wait for the thirty-minute check-in, the desk sergeant would alert one of the Emergency Riders, who would then ride the motorcycle to the call.

On Saturday, May 10, 1924, Officer Webster was on solo vehicle patrol atop the relatively isolated peninsula of Point Loma. According to case notes, his last check-in with headquarters came at approximately 8:30 p.m., when he used the phone at Theosophical Headquarters, the site of what is now Point Loma Nazarene College, at 3900 Lomaland Drive.

Just prior to his phone call, Webster stopped at the security gate of the sprawling ninety-acre cliffside campus to visit with the security guard.

Around 10:00 p.m., fifteen-year-old Henry Silva and fourteen-year-old Robert Herrera reported seeing a dark sedan speed by them

Officer Herbert Webster's official SDPD photo, taken shortly after his return to the department from overseas service during World War I, February 1920. *Courtesy of San Diego Police Museum.*

before it veered off the road and crashed into a patch of weeds. The boys later said they were too scared to approach the machine, so they ran to the home of Harry Sweet at 3786 Tennyson Street. Sweet then notified police.

The emergency call for help came into Police Headquarters at 10:30 p.m. Captain Arthur Hill immediately dispatched Sergeant Robert P. Newsom to the scene. There, Newsom found his badly wounded comrade slumped across the wheel of his car. According to reports, Newsom's first thought was that his comrade had been severely beaten about the face. Detectives later learned that a .25-caliber bullet entered his face below his left eye and lodged at the base of his brain.

Chief of Police James Patrick was notified and began making assignments. Among the first was to determine what happened to Officer Webster. Was a crime committed? If so, where did it occur, and who did it?

They quickly determined that despite being seriously injured with a bullet lodged in his brain, Office Webster had staggered back to his car and tried to drive toward help.

As most of San Diego streets of the era were unpaved, Motorcycle Officers Judson Meade and Ernest Hance were able to follow the tire tracks for almost two miles from the crash. There, at the intersection of Chatsworth Boulevard and an abandoned road, in the soft dirt, were two sets of tire tracks and a pool of blood at the side of the road.

Above: Officer Webster last checked in at a phone on the grounds of the International Theosophical Headquarters. The society ceased to exist decades ago, and the area is now part of Point Loma Nazarene University. *Courtesy of San Diego Police Museum.*

Opposite: The May 13, 1924 *San Diego Union* detailed the shooting of Officer Webster. Despite widespread publicity of one 1924's most shocking cases, no witnesses ever came forward to identify the assailants. *Courtesy of San Diego Police Museum.*

As his fellow policemen scoured the area for clues, a badly wounded Webster was rushed to Police Headquarters at 732 Second Avenue. The headquarters, a long, narrow, two-story clapboard building that served the SDPD from 1911 to 1939, housed an emergency hospital, a police surgeon and nurse and an ambulance.

The on-duty surgeon determined that Webster was suffering from bruising about his head and face. Powder burns indicated the gunshot was fired at very close range.

Given the gravity of his injuries, the badly wounded officer was placed in the police ambulance and rushed to St. Joseph's (now Mercy) Hospital in extremely grave condition. At some point, in a moment of semiconsciousness, Webster muttered, "Seeing the stuff in the car." Detectives later surmised the statement had to do with Webster coming upon a crime in progress when he was shot.

According to police reports, Webster arrived at St. Joseph's in an unconscious state. At his side was fellow Officer Harold Reama, a former U.S. Army nurse with combat experience.

Reama also had personal experience with serious injuries. In 1917, he was leaving headquarters on his police motorcycle when he was run

THE SAN DIEGO UNION: TUESDAY MORNING, MAY 13, 1924

Detectives Have Two Clues That May Solve Mystery Surrounding Attempt to Kill Patrolman Webster

Detectives last night were investigating two clues in an effort to clear up the mystery surrounding the shooting of Patrolman Webster Saturday night. At the top is the junction of an abandoned road and Chatsworth boulevard where the shooting took place. The cross marks the spot where the officer fell. After being shot Webster drove more than two miles before losing consciousness. Tennyson street, second row, is where the officer was found. Left, third row, Patrolman Mead examines Webster's automobile, and right, Patrolman Webster, who is in a critical condition at St. Joseph's hospital. Lower left is a close up of a press car in the exact spot where the officer's auto was found. Right, Patrolmen Hance and Mead examine bloodstains where the officer was shot.

down by a motorist. Hospitalized with a broken neck, Reama was in a cast for months. He remained at the bedside of his wounded comrade for more than a week as Webster hovered near death. The police department would later credit Reama's military training as playing a part in keeping Webster alive.

Within a day of the shooting, the San Diego Police Relief Association (now the San Diego Police Officers Association) established a $250 reward for information leading to the arrest of the assailant or assailants.

Chief Patrick soon increased the fund when he personally offered an additional $50. Within a week, the reward had climbed to $375 after a local citizen and Police Judge Claude Chambers added to it.

As the entire Detective Bureau worked night and day to follow up on leads, on May 13, 1924, the *San Diego Union* reported that the shooting may have been related to "confidential information" Officer Webster received a week earlier. The paper did not mention what information it was, and the police department did not respond to the allegation.

Six days later, on May 19, Webster promised Reama he would "tell him about the shooting, but not tonight." Reama later reported that the rest of Webster's statements were a request for tools to repair his car and frequent mentions of MAin1202 and MAin127, two former phone numbers to the desk sergeant's office that had not been in use for more than a year.

That same day, Police Surgeon E.H. Crabtree, MD, told the *San Diego Union* that he had never heard of anyone surviving a head wound as serious as Webster's. Dr. Crabtree added that surgeons were hesitant to do surgery and were considering leaving the bullet in place.

On May 23, Mr. and Mrs. Peter Blanken phoned Police Headquarters to report that the body of a man, who appeared to be murdered, was lying in a lot next to the road near where Officer Webster had been shot. A carload of patrolmen scrambled to meet Mr. Blanken at the Naval Training Center. After Blanken led the policemen to where he saw the body, they discovered it was gone.

During the ensuing days, Webster managed to relay how he stumbled to his car after being shot and how he tried to summon help from two boys he saw walking along the road. He even recalled crashing his car. What he couldn't provide was the identity of the person who shot him.

On June 6, 1924, Officer Webster told Harold Reama, "I know what happened but I can't frame it into words."

On June 8, the *San Diego Union* reported that Webster's health had taken a turn for the worse when he contracted pneumonia. After his partner's temperature soared to 106 degrees, Reama told the press, "Our only hope is to keep him quiet and we are endeavoring to do so with opiates."

On June 9, detectives met with Mr. Olin Reed of 1335 Third Avenue. Reed reported that he had found an X-ray plate of a human hand in the weeds near where Webster was shot. It was theorized that the plate may have been lost by a passing witness who could offer vital information into the shooting, but it turned out to be just another dead end.

The Police Department thought it finally caught a break on June 11, when Webster was finally strong enough to give a statement. According to the *San Diego Union*, which reported the verbatim conversation, Webster told Reama, "I was driving along Chatsworth Blvd. I saw two fellows monkeying around a car. The engine was going pup pup pup."

"You mean the engine was running?" Reama clarified.

"Yes."

"Then what happened?" Reama asked.

"I told em to get out."

"Then what?"

"We walked down."

"Down where?" Reama pushed.

"To my car. Then I got kicked in the face."

By "kicked" Webster was referring to the actual shooting.

"Did you see the gun?"

"Yes," Webster responded. "It was right before I got kicked."

"Was it a big gun?"

"No, a small one."

"Do you know the fellows?" Reama pushed.

"You and I Harold" was the confusing response. "We'll get em."

If detectives were hoping the descriptor "fellas" would narrow the suspects as male, they were disappointed to learn that since the injury Webster referred to everyone as a "fella," regardless of their gender.

Despite Webster suffering a severe bout of pneumonia just days earlier, on July 26, 1924, doctors publicly declared that he would miraculously survive his injuries. They credited his survival with his exceptional physical condition and to his wife, Jane, who made it a daily routine to visit him and nurse him back to health. Unfortunately, his memory had still not improved to the point where he could provide any additional details as to what had happened.

On November 1, 1924, the San Diego Police Department officially retired Officer Webster at half pay. In 1925, his duty badge, number 22, was reissued to Detective Charles R. Harris.

After receiving his disability pension, Officer Webster and his wife retreated to the Cuyamaca Mountains east of the city for rest.

By 1926, the bullet in Webster's brain was becoming a major issue. The March 2 *San Diego Union* reported that Webster began the year seeming to improve but then was overcome with a series of convulsions. He still could not provide details as to who shot him.

With the recognition that San Diego surgeons didn't have the facilities for such a delicate procedure, Webster was driven to Los Angeles, where he underwent brain surgery on Friday, March 5. The *Union* later reported that the operation was a success. Unfortunately, the good news proved to be temporary, and the next ten years of Webster's life saw his medical condition continue to degrade. The April 5, 1936 *San Diego Union* reported that Officer Webster had his left leg amputated due to nerve damage suffered in the shooting.

In November 1936, Officer Webster sued the police department and the state compensation insurance board for the loss of his leg—something he directly attributed to the shooting. Jane Webster appeared at the deposition on behalf of her husband, as he was hospitalized for the third time since the shooting a dozen years earlier.

Herbert Webster ultimately succumbed to his injuries on January 25, 1951, at Long Beach Veterans Hospital. The next day, the *Union* featured the headline, "Bullet through the Brain Proves Fatal to San Diego Policeman." The *Union* recounted the twenty-six-year-old case and the devastating impact it caused to the Webster family.

Officer Herbert Webster is interred at Fort Rosecrans National Cemetery. He rests just a few thousand yards from where he was critically injured more than a quarter century earlier.

2

AMBUSH IN THE PARK

C harles Rice Harris was born on March 27, 1876, in the rural community of Whitener, Arkansas.

Tall and lanky with a ruddy complexion and ice-blue eyes, Harris was thirty-five years old when he was appointed to the San Diego Police Department, on January 21, 1911.

Charles and his wife, Leona, resided at 3970 J Street in the Stockton neighborhood of San Diego. They had no children, but their niece, Gwendolyn Johnson, born in 1916, lived with them for a time. In a 2002 interview, Gwendolyn described her uncle as one of the kindest, most gentle persons anyone could hope to meet.

Like all new patrolmen, Charles began his police career assigned to uniformed patrol. He then moved to the bicycle squad and the horse-mounted patrol before joining the "Flying Squad" (motorcycles) in 1915. He eventually became a detective.

In 1919, Charles left the department for unknown reasons. It is known that he worked as a motorman (streetcar operator) on the city railway for a period. It was an occupation he had held prior to joining the police department. He rejoined the police department on April 2, 1923.

By 1927, San Diego was growing rapidly. The U.S. Navy had opened a 550-acre Naval Training Center in 1924. Located next to the 110-acre Marine Corps recruit depot, which opened in 1919, the flood of military-related personnel pushed skyward the population of the sleepy Pacific coast hamlet with its mild climate.

The police department had also grown exponentially. In less than forty years, the once small department of a dozen patrolmen had grown to more than 120 officers, detectives, telephone operators and ID Bureau personnel.

In May 1927, the entire world watched Charles Lindbergh fly his silver, purpose-built, single-engine Ryan aircraft monoplane, the *Spirit of St. Louis*, out of San Diego on the first leg of a historic journey that culminated with the world's first solo transatlantic flight, from New York to Paris.

The last known official police department photo of Detective Charles R. Harris before his ambush slaying. *Courtesy of San Diego Police Museum.*

Even that historic event doesn't appear to be untouched by crime. One of the primary builders of the *Spirit of St. Louis*, Frank James, was murdered in April 1951 by his wife, Theodora.

Located just blocks north of downtown is the crown jewel of San Diego, Balboa Park. Set aside as a 1,400-acre "City Park" in 1868, the preserve was little more than canyons, open space and trees until the 1915 Panama-California Exposition put San Diego on the international stage. The yearlong celebration led the park to become home to jogging and hiking trails intermingled with vast lawns, iconic buildings and museums and the world-famous San Diego Zoo.

Despite its incredible beauty, by the 1920s, the park had become a notorious hotbed of crime, vice and sin. The police department became so concerned with hobo encampments and reports of men accosting women, robberies and other crimes in the park that, on August 25, 1925, Matrons Ethel Blair and Carolyn Ettwein were assigned to augment the foot patrol of uniformed policemen already there.

Less than a year later, on April 20, 1926, the department realized that foot patrol was better suited to policewomen with firearms skills, so Olga Nelson and Rena Wright assumed their duties.

It didn't take long for violence to follow.

On January 8, 1927, Policewoman Nelson shot a man who had sprung from the bushes and tried to attack her.

The towering trees and isolated areas of Balboa Park have always made the area a discrete place for lovers to park and get to know each other better. Commonly known as "petting parties," this after-dark activity had been engaged in by several couples when, in the first quarter of 1927, couples

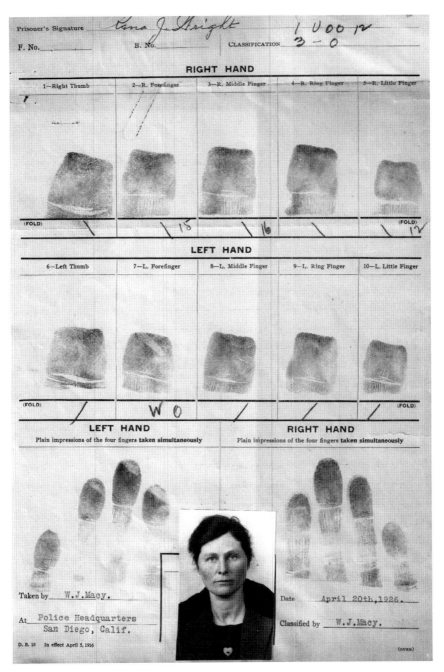

The Charles Harris murder ruined the life of Policewoman Rena Wright. Today, her April 1926 hiring card, containing her photo and fingerprints, is an artifact in the San Diego Police Museum and is all that remains of a once-promising police career. *Courtesy of San Diego Police Museum.*

were accosted by an armed robber who snuck up to the cars and demand cash at gunpoint. The assailant used a flashlight to blind his victims, and by the time anyone could reach a phone to notify the police, the menacing robber was long gone.

How many cases went unreported is anyone's guess. The only description was "an American, 5 feet 11 inches to six feet tall, 160 pounds with a medium complexion, rather full face and well-manicured hands." Not surprisingly, the robber's ambush-style tactics left little physical evidence.

On April 3, 1927, Chief James Patrick directed Detective Harris to partner with Officer Louis Lusk and Policewomen Nelson and Wright to catch the flashlight bandit. Later that day, the group met inside the two-story building that served as the 1915 Exposition police station to devise a plan. Located just west of the iconic California Tower, the old police station building now serves as the administration office for the Museum of Us.

Rena Wright later recounted in her police report, "We were to act as decoys in an attempt to capture the bandit that had been holding up people for some time in the city."

The meeting ended with the officers splitting their operation in two areas. Harris and Wright took the northern section, and Lusk and Olsen covered the south.

According to police reports, Harris and Wright eventually selected "an area of heavy vegetation including Eucalyptus trees, bushes and thick shrubs with paths through the area" near Roosevelt Junior High and the Boy Scout Camp and northwest of "Indian Village"—a holdover exhibit from the 1915 exposition.

Located on what is now the site of the War Memorial Building at 3325 Zoo Drive, the five-acre village was a full-size replica of a Navajo pueblo township common to the old Southwest.

The teams agreed that if they were accosted, the male driver would feign compliance and hold up his hands. Meanwhile, the policewoman would "bring her revolver to bear on the bandit and open fire if necessary."

The plan fell apart, however. As in all of the previous cases, the assailant crept up to the driver's side of the car. But unlike in any previous case, the suspect turned on the flashlight, barked "stick 'em up" and opened fire without warning. Harris was killed instantly.

In an April 4, 1927 police report, Wright stated: "We parked and remained there for about 5–10 minutes and I looked at my watch and said, 'do you think it's about time we called?' He [Harris] said 'yes and we will go now.'

He leaned forward to start the car and at that moment a voice said stick em up, flashed a light in our faces and fired."

Wright's reports detailed what happened next. "As soon as the gunman began shooting Harris exclaimed, 'they got me!'"

Wright responded, "Oh, no, Charlie!" as the gunman fled into the darkness. She did not get out of the car, nor did she shoot at the suspect.

Mortally wounded, Harris slumped to his right across the front seat of the black sedan. Due to their significant size difference, the petite policewoman was unable to pull her partner out of the car. That forced her to push him slightly to one side to start the car.

Seated almost on the passenger side of the car, Wright drove south. The most direct route was down the east–west street that predates modern Richmond Street. Once there, she would have proceeded south on the lonely, one-way Tenth Avenue extension to Police Headquarters at 732 Second Avenue.

The Tenth Avenue extension, just north of the iconic Laurel Street Bridge. Today, the route is the southbound lane of State Highway 163. Northbound Highway 163 lanes were once the Eleventh Avenue extension. *Courtesy of San Diego Police Museum.*

San Diego Police Headquarters, 728 Second Avenue, included an emergency hospital and was staffed by a police surgeon. The building was vacated in 1939 for a much larger facility. The structure was demolished to make way for Horton Plaza in the early 1980s. *Courtesy of San Diego Police Museum.*

According to police reports, Police Surgeon Paul Brust, MD, was on duty that evening, and he pronounced Harris dead on arrival. The postmortem determined that Harris had been shot twice. One shot penetrated the left wrist. The fatal shot was through the chest. Powder burns around the wrist wound led investigators to surmise that Harris had raised his arm at one point.

As events were unfolding downtown, the lack of a police radio left the second undercover team on the south end of the park completely unaware of what had happened.

After Chief of Police James Patrick was briefed, he and several officers, including Policewoman Wright, returned to Balboa Park for what ultimately proved to be an unfruitful search.

According to reports, later that evening, Rena Wright accompanied Detective Sergeant John Kane, to the Harris's home, where they "acquainted Mrs. Harris with the death of her husband." As Kane and Wright consoled Mrs. Harris, Chief Patrick ordered all available officers, including those off duty, to return to work.

Standing before an assembly of his officers Chief Patrick ordered: "That man must be brought in and I don't want to see him alive. Bring him in. Don't ask any questions. Shoot and shoot fast."

The Chief then detailed all uniformed patrolmen to participate in the park search. Detectives were commanded to coordinate the investigation, review all evidence and interview suspects.

As the patrolmen fanned out into the darkness to search the massive park, a team of investigators led by Captain of Detectives Harry Kelly huddled at Police Headquarters to pore over any possible clues that would lead them to the deadly triggerman.

Kelly's investigators came to believe the killer was the same individual who had robbed Monroe Cooper and his female companion on April 2 near Indian Village.

According to police reports, Cooper and a female companion were driving slowly along Upas Street when a man wearing a brown sweater and an army hat jumped on the car's running board and thrust a gun at them. "All right buddy, stick 'em up!" the robber snarled.

Cooper said he stopped and turned off the motor. As the couple sat helpless with the gun trained on them, the bandit demanded to see their hands to check for rings. Finding nothing, he ordered Cooper to "wait a few minutes to start his car." The robber then fled south into the park. His description matched those in prior robberies.

As the investigators reviewed the previous robbery cases, one of the biggest questions facing them was why the suspect had deviated from prior robberies, which did not involve gunfire. One theory was that he may have recognized Harris or Wright. Given that Wright walked a beat in the park, it was plausible that someone prowling that area could have recognized her.

A second theory was that the robber could have been someone Harris had previously arrested. It was also theorized the triggerman might have overheard them speaking as he crept up on the vehicle.

If the case was to be solved, a veteran investigator like Captain Kelly knew that his men needed to investigate every angle.

On April 4, the coroner, Schuyler G. Kelly, convened a twelve-man inquest led by foreman Fred B. Groves. Among the witnesses appearing before the jury were Policewomen Wright and Nelson, Patrolman Lusk and autopsy surgeon Joseph J. Shea.

The findings of the inquest were as follows: "That he came to his death on the 3rd day of April, AD, 1927, in San Diego County California, hemorrhage from a bullet wound of Aorta. We the jury find that said wound was inflicted by a bullet fired from a revolver in the hands of an unknown party with homicidal intent."

While the homicide verdict was predictable, most of the testimony of Policewoman Wright, a member of the SDPD for less than a year, was anything but. Wright stated that she and Harris had been vigilant about looking back and around the car constantly in case someone approached, but that they never saw anyone.

Then things took a strange twist. The inquest report stated that Wright was "unable to provide any accurate description of what happened or provide the make or caliber of the gun she was carrying." According to reports, she also didn't know where her firearm currently was.

Wright's testimony that she didn't hear Harris fire his weapon was contradicted by an investigator's report that detailed that his weapon was fired five times and had been recovered on the driver's side floor. One round had lodged into the wood molding on the door interior.

Meanwhile, Chief Patrick needed to address the public outcry for more police protection in the park. The Chief explained that he had already detailed two policewomen and two patrolmen to park patrol. He added that he had assigned two officers to patrol after Policewomen Wright and Olsen were done with their watch at 10:00 p.m.

On a larger note, Patrick said that the department had only twenty-five patrol officers to cover ninety square miles of city and 1,400 acres in Balboa Park. "The police department has not had an adequate force since I have been connected with it during the last 15 years" the Chief declared.

Shortly after the shooting, Mr. J.A. Foster came forward to volunteer the use of his two bloodhounds. Detective Sergeant Richard Chadwick put the dogs on the scent at the location of the shooting. He later reported that the dogs led officers on several trails, but none "panned out."

Case file notes reflect that Motorcycle Officer Mike Neely spent two days riding over two hundred miles through the backcountry to locate possible clues. On his second day, he tried to track down a lead that a man fitting the suspect's description had driven through the backcountry and to Lake Hodges only an hour or two after Harris had been killed.

Captain Arthur Hill later reported that the man Neely was looking for had actually left the city some time before the killing.

An April 7, 1927 report indicates that Detective Sergeant Kane interviewed Karl Kilgore, an employee at the San Diego Zoo, as a possible suspect. Kilgore said he was with his girlfriend on the night of the murder. Detectives later verified the alibi.

Kane also interviewed zoo foreman Norman Johnson, who said that on the night Harris was killed he "heard shots" but didn't pay attention, because he thought he was hearing car backfires.

After receiving a tip that John C. Allen, a night watchman at the zoo, had recently been seen wearing a brown sweater, detectives brought him in for questioning. Case notes reflect that Allen "proved beyond a doubt" that he had nothing to do with the murder.

Policewoman Nelson reported that she knew of two men living in the Boy Scout headquarters and that she "didn't know what they did." After police located two teachers who were living at the camp, both were questioned.

H.L. Kimball was one of the men. He told detectives that he served as the principal at the Garfield School. He identified the other man as R.M Linscheid, a teacher at the Jefferson school.

Kimball said that on the night of the shooting he had been to a party with his girlfriend at her sister's home. He stated that he was sitting at a desk when he heard shots. He said he then heard a siren and "was satisfied something had happened." Harris's unmarked car had a siren, but it was never determined if that was the one Kimball heard.

After questioning Kimball, the detective decided "he was very much a gentleman and didn't seem putout" by the questioning. The man was released.

As detectives worked the biggest case of 1927, numerous patrolmen swept filling stations, garages, rooming houses, restaurants and "any place where people were around at night" when the shooting had occurred. Nothing of consequence was located.

After receiving information that Edward Wright was the park bandit, prior victims were contacted and shown his photo, but no one made an identification. After learning that Wright had a criminal record, Chief Patrick wired San Quentin Prison requesting additional information. They learned that Wright had been sent to an out-of-state prison and was incarcerated when Harris was killed.

Acting on a tip that Ralph Dumont was the park bandit, Detective Sergeant Kane drove to the old town pumping plant, where Dumont worked. He was told that Dumont "had left town two months after cleaning out the man he was staying with."

Detectives showed Dumont's photo to witnesses, but no one was able to make a positive identification.

On April 17, 1927, J.D. Stanley, a sailor assigned to Naval Air Station North Island, was held up by an unmasked robber. It was the first stickup since the Harris murder fourteen days earlier.

The robbery occurred shortly after Stanley stepped off a streetcar at Seventeenth and Broadway and was walking north on the east side of the street toward his home at 1219 Seventeenth Street. He was about midblock when a tall man stepped from behind a garage and leveled a .38-caliber blue-steel revolver at his heart and said, "Stick up your hands." The robber searched Stanley and took thirty dollars from his watch pocket. He then fled north into Balboa Park.

That same day, the *San Diego Union* published an open letter from Mrs. Harris. Despite being in poor health, the widow thanked everyone who had assisted her in her time of sorrow and bereavement.

On April 20, 1927, Motorcycle Officer Robert Jump arrested George Fraser after observing Fraser driving erratically. Believing Fraser resembled the description of the park bandit, Jump arrested him. Fraser was released the following day after it was determined that he "was not close enough" to the description of the suspect.

On April 22, there was another park robbery, this time at Thirteenth and Olive Streets, an area that intersected the park on the east side. In that case, E.L. Changon had just stepped off a streetcar when a man sprang from behind a concrete wall.

"Stick 'em up" the robber demanded while brandishing a small semi-automatic handgun. "I mean business. Straighten up or I'll slap you alongside your head." When the robbery was interrupted by the headlights of an approaching vehicle, the suspect fled into Balboa Park.

According to detective notes, the suspect bore a resemblance to the robber in the earlier cases and in the murder of Harris.

In May 1927, Denver, Colorado Police Chief Robert Reed notified the SDPD that they had a mentally deranged man named Gary Dolbow, aka James Keen, in their custody. According to the Chief, Dolbow admitted to two "petting party stickups" in Balboa Park and a holdup of a pedestrian in La Jolla. Dolbow also claimed he saw Detective Harris shot by another stickup man "in his 20's."

The claim of having witnessed Harris being shot was contradicted by more than a score of San Diego Police officers, who declared that they knew the exact spot where Harris's "machine" had been parked. They were unanimous in the belief that a man could not have seen the shooting or the slayer that night unless he was standing directly alongside or had fired the shots himself.

Detective Sergeant Kane determined that Dolbow had lived in San Diego at the Angelus Hotel at Fourth and C Streets in early January 1927 until shortly after Harris was shot, But the killing Dolbow was referring to was most likely the murder of August Richter on March 28, 1927.

In the Richter case, the robbers had carjacked a vehicle from E.J. Pritchard in the 1700 block of Sixth Street on the west side of Balboa Park. The suspects used the stolen car during the robbery and murder of Richter at Arizona Street and El Cajon Boulevard, ten blocks north of Balboa Park.

According to Richter's female companion, the couple was sitting in his car when two men approached asking directions to the U.S. Grant Hotel. When Richter saw a revolver in the hand of one of the robbers, he sprang from the car just as the second robber lunged for her.

The surviving witness stated that Richter tackled the gunman and then grabbed a stick from near the front seat and hit him over the head. The robber then stepped back and shot Richter in the abdomen.

Witnesses reported a second man, possibly Dolbow, was in the background when Richter was shot. As the robbers fled in the stolen car, the female saw a third man inside.

At first, it seemed the information about Dolbow was the break the cops needed, especially considering that a partial report from the Coroner's Office stated that the bullet that killed Richter was fired from the same gun that killed Harris.

Officer Lewis Lusk (*third from right*) and other members of the SDPD machine squad in the 1920s. Like Charles Harris, Lusk met an untimely end in Balboa Park. *Courtesy of San Diego Police Museum.*

However, a report filed by Harry Kelly stated, in part: "Detective Kane also took the bullet found in Harris' body and those found in Richter, to Los Angeles. The bullets were calibrated and enlarged photos were taken and found that they were not fired by the same gun."

Detective Charles Harris was laid to rest on April 8, 1927. His services were held at the Masonic temple with more than one hundred officers in attendance. He was interred at Mount Hope Cemetery.

On September 30, 1928, Balboa Park claimed another policeman when Lewis Lusk suffered a massive heart attack while on patrol near the Cabrillo Bridge. Rushed to St. Joseph's, Lusk died shortly thereafter. At the time of his death, Lusk wore badge number 11. The number is half of 22, the badge number of Charles Harris and Herbert Webster.

Several years after the Harris killing, various individuals were identified as possible suspects, but none were charged.

To date, Detective Harris and Officer Herbert Webster are the only San Diego Police officers to be victims of an unsolved, line-of-duty murder.

3

INNOCENCE STOLEN

FEBRUARY 11, 1931.

It was shortly after 8:00 a.m. when ten-year-old Virginia Brooks left a small stack of unfinished handmade Valentine cards on the dining room table to walk one and a third miles to Euclid Elementary School at 4166 Euclid Avenue. She was clutching a bouquet of wild flowers to give to her teacher when she merrily skipped out the door.

According to her mother, Blanche, the slender, blue-eyed brunette with a radiant smile left the modest family home at 5602 University Avenue wearing a little white dress, short socks and a brown coat.

The last person to see Virginia was her twelve-year-old brother Gordon, who rode by on his bicycle and waved as she leisurely walked west along what was then a sparsely populated, lazy, tree-lined University Avenue.

When she didn't return home after school, her parents notified the East San Diego police substation. Lieutenant Robert Newsom was the station commander and took the initial report. He then directed Detective Sergeant George Cooley and Officer A.R. Rodefer to respond to the Brooks home and begin a search of the neighborhood. When they found nothing, more than two dozen uniformed patrolmen were brought in from across the city for a door-to-door search and a search of nearby canyons.

Police later learned that Virginia was supposed to meet a schoolmate, Kathy Lucero, halfway between home and school. According to Kathy, Virginia never showed up.

Despite searching through the night, police found no sign of Virginia.

The next morning, detectives searched an abandoned, 125-foot well partially filled with quicklime three miles from the Brooks home. They found nothing.

As news of the missing girl spread, so did alleged sightings. Each tip was pursued, but they all proved either a case of mistaken identity or inconclusive.

Within days, the search had spread as far as Arizona and Oregon.

Some local media compared the disappearance to that of eleven-year-old

Frances Marion Parker, who was kidnapped and brutally murdered in Los Angeles in 1927. The *Los Angeles Times* dubbed the Parker case "the most horrible crime of the 1920s." The *Visalia Times* went further, labeling it "the most horrific crime in California history."

While there were similarities, there were also significant differences. Parker was the daughter of an established, wealthy Los Angles banker, and a ransom had been made. Virginia was the daughter of a modest, working-class family that had just moved to San Diego from Portland, Oregon.

Detectives in San Diego knew there was no way the cases were related; like every police agency in Southern California, they had been a part of the Los Angeles Police Department manhunt and were aware that Frances Parker's killer, nineteen-year-old William Edward Hickman, was hanged in the San Quentin gallows in October 1928.

Within a week, the high-profile nature of the crime, indexed as case C4286, had Chief of Police Arthur Hill personally heading the investigation. At that time, Chief Hill told the press that his investigators had pieced together enough information to determine that Virginia was kidnapped by someone in an automobile within four blocks of her house. Days later, detectives located a man who admitted to previously giving rides to Virginia, but he was able to establish an alibi, having been with six other men on the day she went missing.

In mid-March, Chief Hill received a letter with a San Diego postmark. Contained within the letter, written half in cursive and half in block letters, was not only a confession to killing Brooks but also a threat. "I have defied your experts! Ha! Ha! Another schoolgirl will disappear within a week! Let

Opposite: The innocent smile of Virginia Brooks shortly before her still-unsolved murder case set the city of San Diego on its head. *Courtesy of San Diego Police Museum.*

Above: The Brooks case occupied most of the daily headlines in 1931.

mothers and parents beware! Virginia was attacked before death not after she died. That shows how little your experts know!" The letter was signed "The Gorilla."

Los Angeles Criminologist Rex Welch examined the letter and concluded that it was most likely written by the same person who penned a previous confession a few days earlier. In that letter, the author identified himself as "The Doctor."

As the case approached the one-month mark, detectives were no closer to solving it than on the day Virginia went missing. Despite a seven-days-a-week work schedule and following up on dozens of alleged sightings and interviewing scores of potential witnesses or suspects, investigators were looking at a stone wall. They needed a break.

It came on March 10, 1931, when shepherd George H. Moses was walking his collie, Blackie, in a lonely, windswept area of the abandoned Camp Kearny Mesa, a 12,700-acre U.S. Army mobilization and training facility that had been used for troops on their way to the European battlefields

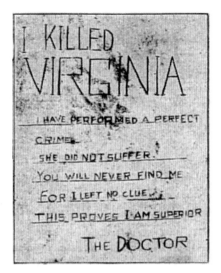

A crude correspondence from the "Doctor" was one of several false confessions to surface during the Brooks case. The letters were huge distractions to an overworked Detective Bureau charged with verifying their authenticity. The perpetrator of the cruel hoax was never identified.

of World War I. Originally named in honor of Brigadier General Stephen W. Kearny, a leader in the Mexican-American War who also served as a military governor of California, the area today is part of USMCAS Miramar.

According to the *San Diego Union*, it was shortly after 11:00 a.m. when Blackie stopped, sniffed the air and then began barking madly toward a small berm. Moses investigated and discovered a burlap sack that appeared to contain a small human body. Moses sprinted toward the highway and flagged down a passing truck. "Telephone the sheriff's office!" he shouted at the startled trucker. "I've found a body."

The truck driver raced south, to Old Town, where he found a phone and notified authorities. At the scene within a half hour were Deputy Sheriffs Blake Mason and Jack Tillery; Deputy Coroner Dave Gershon, who was also a former SDPD Detective and former special agent of the Bureau of Investigation (now known as the FBI); Chief Hill; and a score of officers and newspapermen in dark suits and fedora hats.

Moses led the group to his discovery behind a small mound of dirt a half mile east of Murray Canyon Road which served as the inland San Diego–Los Angeles highway.

Investigator notes detail that the remote location made it possible for the killer to discard the sack without being seen by passing motorists. It was very close to the place where the skeleton of thirteen-year-old Nicholas Esparza of 4329 Copeland Avenue was discovered by a hunter named Clyde B. Linden on September 18, 1927.

It had been a month since the four-foot, six-inch, seventy-five-pound girl had gone missing. The condition of the body suggested that she had probably been killed within hours of being kidnapped.

Detective case notes referenced that "a strange and quick working acid" had been poured on the body, possibly to destroy evidence. A postmortem report by Dr. Frank Toomey of the Coroner's Office later refuted the theory.

A half mile of thin tire tracks in the mud suggested that a "light weight automobile" with over-inflated tires had transported Virginia to the remote area. Detectives later determined the tracks came from a very common tire manufactured by the Joe Shelley Tire Company, a manufacturer/wholesaler at 1031 Market Street. The Shelly Company supplied tire dealers across the region, making it virtually impossible to track down the private customer who purchased them.

At first, a plaster casting of tire tracks near where Virginia's body was found seemed to be a valuable piece of evidence. The lead fell apart when it was discovered how common the tire was. *Courtesy of San Diego Police Museum.*

The lack of discoloration of the grass under the bag, coupled with the speed at which the grass sprang upright when the bag was lifted, suggested that Virginia had been there less than twelve hours. The timeline was affirmed by Moses, who stated that he had his dog with him a few days earlier when he was shooting tin cans. A bullet-riddled can recovered nearby verified the story.

Approximately twelve feet from the body was another burlap sack, this one containing figures and advertisements cut from local 1927 newspapers as well as three library books matching those Virginia had when she set out for school. One of the books contained what the press described as "a glazed page" and partial prints left by a thumb and forefinger.

The limits of forensic science at the time rendered a hand search for a fingerprint the metaphorical "needle in a haystack," But Identification Bureau Superintendent Walter Macy checked the partial prints among the department's extensive collection of known suspects' inked cards. He failed to locate a positive match. An attempt to develop fingerprints on the shiny, black leather shoes Virginia had been wearing also fell short due to the limits of the science.

After inspecting the crime scene with Chief Hill, Chief of Detectives Paul Hayes told the press, "We're closing in on the killer and expect to have him in custody within 24 hours." Meanwhile, Chief Hill drove to the Brooks home, where he notified the family of their little girl's fate.

Word of the slaying spread fast. According to the *Idaho Statesman*, police guards had to be posted at the Brooks home after "morbid crowds rushed to the house of sorrow" to intrude on the family and steal souvenirs. The *Statesman* also reported that a small garden Virginia had planted was trampled by the mob before the police could arrive.

According to the *San Francisco Examiner*, the family took the news hard. Clutching the Valentine cards her daughter had been making, Mrs. Brooks reportedly said, "I'll try and bear it but I don't know....I'm afraid I can't stand it," before collapsing.

Mr. Brooks responded with rage. "If I could catch the man who did it, I'd tear his throat out."

Later that day, detectives searched a vacant building and barn near Thirty-Fourth and F Streets, where a newspaper and a burlap sack had been located. They found nothing related to the Brooks killing.

As uniformed patrolmen contacted seventy known "degenerates" across the city, detectives were at Police Headquarters feverishly combing through the Nicholas Esparza murder file for similarities to the Virginia Brooks case.

According to the March 11, 1931 *San Diego Evening Tribune*, Gordon Stewart Northcott, who was later revealed to be the "Wineville Chicken Farm Slayer," had been brought to San Diego and questioned by detectives after matching the general description of the man Nicholas was last seen with on May 28, 1927, shortly after 11:00 a.m.

Northcott had confessed to killing Esparza, who was last seen with a man in a blue car near Young's Caves, a series of subterranean passages at the foot of Fairmount Street in Mission Valley. Dug by a recluse in the early 1920s, by the time the caves were dynamited in the 1930s to seal off public access, they had become a notorious meeting place for "bad characters."

Whether Northcott was telling the truth was another issue. He had confessed to a number of Southland murders but then, in some cases, could not answer specific questions about the crime or withdrew his confession altogether.

Detectives would not get a second interview. The Canadian serial killer was hanged in San Quentin on October 2, 1930, for the murder of three preteens— Alvin Gothea and brothers Lewis and Nelson Winslow—on his Wineville, California ranch. Police throughout Southern California believed that Northcott and his mother, Sarah, may have killed up to twenty young boys.

The citizens of Wineville were so traumatized by Northcott that they changed the name of the community to Mira Loma on

Serial killer George Stewart Northcott confessed to a San Diego child murder, but he had already been hanged by the time the body of Virginia Brooks was found in the same place as his victim, fourteen-year-old Nick Esparza, was recovered in 1927.

November 1, 1930, only a month after his execution. Today, Mira Loma is known as Jurupa Valley.

In 2008, Clint Eastwood profiled Northcott and the March 1928 kidnapping of ten-year-old Walter Collins in his critically acclaimed crime drama *Changeling*.

Dr. Toomey conducted the postmortem of Virginia Brooks. In his report, he stated his belief that the cause of death was strangulation by a makeshift tourniquet around her neck. Advanced decomposition indicated that the killing most likely occurred shortly after she had been abducted.

When it was revealed that some of Virginia's organs had been removed, Chief Hayes instructed his men to look for suspects with possible surgical experience and to check locations for a possible laboratory where the killing might have taken place.

News of the finding spread quickly. Joseph Taylor, Chief of Detectives of the Los Angeles Police Department, offered the assistance of investigators, chemists and fingerprint experts if they were needed.

On March 13, Chief Hill received an anonymous letter stating that Virginia had been a sacrificial victim and that the killing of Nicholas Esparza was related. "The murder is not the work of a degenerate man as believed," the letter stated. "If you look for a black magic adept, seeker of a hidden treasure, you will probably work on the right track. This man is without the doubt the man who killed the Esparza boy in 1927 and lives in that neighborhood."

Chief Hill ultimately dismissed the letter as that of a crank.

Virginia was laid to rest on Saturday, March 21, in Mount Hope Cemetery. The City of San Diego donated the burial plot. More than four thousand people, many of whom had never met the girl or her family, attended the service. As the eulogy was delivered, mixed with prayers for the police to solve the case, undercover bureau men stood within the crowd, looking for any sign that the killer was in attendance.

That same day, Lieutenant Sears announced another letter from the Gorilla, the second in two days. Left on a car near Park Boulevard and Madison Avenue, the note read, "Beware! Gorilla will get you next!" Sears noted that the handwriting did not match that of the previous letter and considered it to be the work "of a crank."

By now, bureau men had interviewed hundreds of possible suspects. They had also visited almost every garage and tire shop in the city, looking for a match to the muddy tracks left at the scene. Despite the exhaustive effort, they were no closer to solving the case than when it began.

The State of California also offered investigators. While the help was eagerly welcomed, the results were the same. There was simply not enough evidence to make a case.

On April 21, John Brooks appeared at the SDPD's East San Diego substation asking that he either be locked up for the night or have a guard posted at his home. According to John, a local radio broadcaster falsely suggested that he had killed his daughter after discovering he was not her father.

Several East San Diego newspapers even went so far as to report men throughout the community were meeting and voicing suggestions that "they ought to go out and get the ———."

Rumors that John killed Virginia had existed since the little girl went missing. They intensified as police ran out of suspects, but there was no proof that John had anything to do with the crime, and detectives never considered him as a suspect.

On May 10, 1931, fifty-six-year-old Jack McVane was arrested after his remote Del Dios cabin was raided by a task force of state investigators, members of the San Diego and Los Angeles Police Departments and San Diego County Deputy Sheriff Blake Mason. Described by the *San Diego Union* as an "eccentric recluse," McVane had lived for eight years in a three-room shack he built on a 640-acre tract of land five miles west of Lake Hodges.

Investigators had been tipped off after McVane boasted of once being in the death house at San Quentin. According to those who knew him, McVane was a "nice man but had a hair trigger temper" and would threaten to "blow their heads off" if he discovered they were police.

Inside the home was a paper tablet blotter with the scrawled name "Virginia" with a heart drawn next to it. According to the *San Diego Evening Tribune*, the writing appeared to be "from a child's hand."

In addition to recovering a stash of weapons, including knives and a machine gun, from a shrub-covered hideout cabin four miles from his main home, detectives noted that McVane had access to a dark blue coupe similar to one seen by neighbors near the Brooks home on the day little Virginia went missing.

A fingerprint check confirmed that the arrestee was actually Richard M. Ward, a convicted double murderer who had escaped from Folsom Prison on January 23, 1921. A jockey by vocation, the slightly built Ward was first incarcerated in 1893 after murdering a fellow jockey with a pitchfork. Sentenced to life in prison, he was released in 1903, only to be back in prison for murder in 1911 after he beat a coworker to death.

Ward was questioned extensively by Undersheriff Oliver Sexson but was cleared as a suspect in the Brooks killing before being returned to Folsom Prison. Months later, more than four hundred people signed a petition to the governor demanding a pardon for his crimes.

On December 9, 1934, Blanche Brooks died following a botched surgery. John, now widowed, and his two sons, Gordon and George, left San Diego.

Four years had transpired when, on March 3, 1935, the Detective Bureau received word that after spending twenty-four hours in the city jail on a drunk charge, thirty-two-year-old Joseph Mieler confessed to killing Virginia. "I hit her in the head with a rock and then shot her with a revolver," Mieler told jail staff.

Detectives met with Mieler and, after determining it was a false confession, filed an insanity charge against him.

Meanwhile, despite investigators questioning a line of possible suspects, by the end of the 1930s, the case had gone dormant. There simply were no more leads to chase. Then, on January 2, 1946, forty-two-year-old U.S.

Navy Chief Petty Officer Dennis Stroud contacted the San Diego Police Department with an incredible story.

Stroud told Detective Lieutenant Ed Dieckmann, District Attorney Thomas Whelan and Inspector Fred Christensen that a man named Owen Jack Hayes killed Virginia Brooks fifteen years earlier.

According to the case report, Stroud told the men he was in the U.S. Navy and stationed in San Diego in 1931. "Hayes was a bootlegger and I was one of his customers and I went to his home from time to time," Stroud said. "About March 20 I was at Hayes home and I noticed he was upset. I started drinking with him and we talked together."

Detectives noted that Hayes had lived at 4276 Altadena Street in 1931. The home was less than two miles from the Brooks residence.

Stroud continued, "That's when Hayes asked me, 'if you were on parole from Oregon and you accidently killed that little girl, what would you do?'"

Stroud said, "I replied I suppose I would have done what the killer did."

According to Stroud, Hayes said, "Well that's what I did."

Stroud added that Hayes told him, "I was driving my truck. I couldn't stop and I hit her. Then I stopped, picked up her body and put it in a gunny sack. I drove it out to the mesa and left it there."

Stroud said his story could be corroborated by Tony Cito, a fellow sailor he once served with. According to Stroud, Cito was with him when Hayes confessed and that they discussed the case as they made their way back to the ship. Stroud said when he asked Cito what they should do with the information, Cito replied, "I'd forget all about it."

"Why did you wait so long to come forward?" Lieutenant Dieckmann asked.

"It's been bothering me for a long time. I needed to get it off my conscience. When I was overseas I spoke to a friend of mine who was a former Los Angeles policeman. He told me to come forward."

Detectives later identified the former policeman as J.W. Vance, an SDPD applicant. When detectives spoke to him, Vance confirmed that Stroud told him the same story twice—"word for word"—while they were stationed in Sardinia, Italy, in 1944. Vance said he and Stroud agreed that whoever made it back to the United States first would contact the police.

According to the San Diego Police Museum's all-time service roster, despite being certified as eligible for employment, Vance was never hired as an SDPD officer.

On February 1, 1946, Jack Hayes drove more than five hundred miles from Sacramento to San Diego to turn himself in for questioning. Shortly after being taken into custody, Hayes issued a statement through his attorney insisting that he voluntarily surrendered after learning he was wanted. Hayes's attorney then added to the statement, insisting his client had been implicated by Stroud because Stroud was seeking revenge on his client. The attorney did not reveal what the issue was.

According to the case file, Lieutenant Dieckmann and Inspector Christensen interviewed Hayes. While he readily admitted to bootlegging during Prohibition, he emphatically denied having anything to do with the horrific crime. "I wouldn't hurt a soul" Hayes insisted.

Hayes added that on the day Virginia went missing, he was making a whiskey delivery to two prominent El Centro residents. "I might get them to establish an alibi," Hayes declared, "but maybe they won't like their names brought into anything like this."

Hayes then turned the interview around and asked the policemen why it took so long for Stroud to reach out. "I'm no stool pigeon," Hayes insisted, "but if anyone had told me they'd committed a crime of that type I would have gone to the police immediately and turned him in."

Despite Hayes's denials, on Saturday February 2, 1946, District Attorney Whelan told the press, "I'm convinced Stroud is telling the truth. His statements corroborate much of the testimony given at the inquest." Whelan was referring to testimony from Walter E. Bell, a watchman at a downtown hotel.

Bell, a resident of El Cajon, told the inquest jury that he drove by the Brooks home on the morning that Virginia vanished. Bell said he noticed a Model A pickup (of the type allegedly driven by Hayes) pass the house at the time.

Doctor Toomey's reports made it clear he didn't share the District Attorney's enthusiasm. He had already declared strangulation as the cause of death. There were no bruises or broken bones on Virginia's body to support the theory that she had been struck by a vehicle. Toomey added that pieces of the girl's clothing had been intertwined with a stick to form a tourniquet-like garrot and that was what was used to kill her.

On February 3, 1946, the police department received word that Hayes had attempted to hang himself in his jail cell. Dieckmann ordered Detective Elmer Wadman to go to the County Jail and interview Hayes as to why.

"Is it true you tried to stretch your neck?" Wadman asked.

"Yes," Hayes responded. "I'm tired of being questioned."

The *San Diego Union* reported that later that same evening, Chief of Police Clifford Peterson and Lieutenant Dieckmann questioned Hayes, only this time he denied trying to kill himself. "I'm not the type to try anything like that!" Hayes insisted.

Investigators then learned that Ernest Zumaya, quartered in a cell near Hayes, had twice tried to take his own life and that jail staff had confused the two men.

Despite the serious misgivings of the medical examiner, on February 5, 1946, Hayes was arraigned for the murder of Virginia Brooks.

The *San Diego Union* reported that Hayes walked into his court appearance looking confident and smiling. The paper stated that the tall, slender, balding defendant seemed unmoved as Judge A.F. Molina read the complaint and then ordered him remanded to jail to face a preliminary hearing on February 27.

On Monday, February 26, the entire case fell apart when District Attorney Whelan told the court that Dennis Stroud had declined to accept the subpoena to appear at the February 27 prelim. Whelan then presented a telegram that read: "Unable to obtain authority to temporarily transfer Dennis Dent Stroud, CBM, USN, as witness....Sheriff's Office San Francisco informed of man's declination to accept subpoena." The telegram was signed, "Receiving Station, Treasure Island."

Whelan told the court, "If Stroud isn't available for the prelim there's nothing we can do but release Hayes and dismiss the charge."

Stroud's refusal to accept the subpoena prompted the media to question how he could refuse it. District Attorney Whelan explained that anyone on a government reservation could refuse a subpoena for a civilian court.

Stroud later told investigators that his commanding officer would not release him from duty and that he didn't want to go AWOL.

After learning that charges were being dropped, Hayes told the *San Diego Union*, "Of course I'm pleased to learn Stroud now doesn't see fit to come here to testify against me. His whole statement was a prefabrication without any grounds to substantiate it."

Hayes added that several people had sent him money for a legal defense but he didn't accept it. Hayes added that he was sorry he didn't have information to help solve the Brooks murder.

After Jack Hayes was released on February 28, District Attorney Whelan filed charges against Stroud for giving police false and misleading statements. He was booked after being unable to post a $1,000 bond.

At the March 11, 1946 arraignment, Whelan told Judge Molina that Hayes was willing to testify against Stroud. On March 30, 1946, charges were dropped and Stroud was remanded to the navy for disciplinary action.

District Attorney Whelan told the press that after interviewing Stroud, he was convinced the Chief Petty Officer was motivated to incriminate Hayes for the reward that had been offered.

Who killed Virginia Brooks is still a mystery. As they retired, more than one career law enforcement officer stated that the Brooks case was the one that would haunt them forever.

In a 1960 interview, Lieutenant Ed Dieckmann, now retired, said he was proud of the SDPD Homicide Bureau's 96 percent rate of solving cases but that he, too, lamented the case not being solved.

The 1967 obituary for Deputy Blake Mason recounted many of the high-profile cases and gun battles he was involved in during his storied career. The obituary correctly credited him as being one of the best lawmen in San Diego County history, but the narrative incorrectly stated that he played a part in solving the Virginia Brooks case.

4

LOUISE TEUBER

APRIL 19, 1931.

Lemon Grove sheepherder Toney Martinez and his family were hiking through the small wooded grove at the base of Black Mountain, searching for the perfect spot for a casual Sunday picnic.

Their plans for a peaceful outing were shattered when they stumbled upon the body of a young woman hanging in an oak tree. She was clad only in thigh-high stockings and black pumps. A wool U.S. Army blanket had been spread beneath her body. With her heels touching the ground and knees bent forward, she appeared to be in an almost elevated seated position.

A black, fur-trimmed coat, a light-blue silk skirt, a white blouse and female underclothing were folded neatly nearby.

Mrs. Martinez raced to a telephone to summon the Sheriff. Deputies John Stevens and Charles Cameron, along with La Mesa Police Chief B.L. Mercer, responded.

The scene was just west of the four-hundred-foot *S* recently painted to memorialize nearby San Diego State College (now known as San Diego State University). Today, the location is known as Cowles Mountain. The expansion of municipal boundaries over time now place it in the city of San Diego and under the jurisdiction of the San Diego Police Department.

Deputies noted several yards of drag marks toward the tree, where a large letter *I* had been carved into the base. They also noted that the oily, worn rope around the victim's neck had been thrown over a tree branch and the other end lashed to a stump almost twenty feet away. Friction burns on the branch suggested the body had been hoisted into position.

According to preliminary reports, the death knot had been skillfully tied in a double half-hitch and the line was consistent with a hammock lash used by sailors.

Injuries to the young woman's body included fingernail marks to one of her ears and her neck, collar abrasions caused by the rope and bruises on her back and shoulders. Estimates were that she had been dead eight hours before the horrific discovery.

A set of fresh tire tracks near the tree was photographed, and the clothing and rope were collected as evidence.

With the Virginia Brooks case still dominating local headlines, the news of another mysterious death spread like wildfire. To help Sheriff Edgar Cooper's investigators, Chief of Police Arthur Hill detailed five men from the SDPD Detective Bureau to assist.

FOUND SLAIN

Here is one of the last photographs ever taken of Louise Teuber, 17, San Diego girl, who was found hanged on Black Mountain.

The body was carefully cut down and then transported to the Fred Erickson Funeral Home in La Mesa where the girl was identified as seventeen-year-old Louise M. Teuber of 4049 Vermont Street. A student of the E.R. Snyder Continuation School, Louise lived with her father, William, a local barber, and her grandparents.

William, who raised Louise as a single father since the death of her mother in 1916, was distraught. He told detectives that he last saw Louise on Thursday, April 16, when they quarreled about her going out.

William said Louise worked at the S.H. Kress Five and Dime at 1038 Fifth Avenue. A follow-up with her supervisor, Dora Sena, revealed that Louise began working there in June 1930 but that she resigned on Saturday, April 18, after telling coworkers she was moving to Seattle. According to Sena, she paid Louise $11.65, the balance of her wages, and Louise left the store.

When asked about how Louise got home after leaving work, a coworker, Myretta Farris, said Louise's manner of transportation was evenly split

The cruel murder of "spirited" teen Louise Teuber set the city into a frenzy. Residents of the small sleepy navy town of San Diego began considering the possibility of a serial killer.

between riding the streetcars and going home in autos with friends. Farris added that when she last saw Louise, on Saturday at 5:30 p.m., Louise was not of a despondent nature and seemed in good spirits.

Another coworker stated that Louise told her she would be leaving for Chicago on Sunday, April 19, but that she wanted to attend a party at the library on Saturday evening.

Then came a bombshell. According to Blanche Webb, another Kress coworker, Louise was married to a sailor on the USS *West Virginia* based in the Los Angeles Harbor and had frequently spoke of her secret marriage. "Louise told me, 'When I work a little longer and save some money, I'm going to join my husband,'" Webb said. Even though Louise claimed to be married, Webb added that she went out with "a number of young men."

According to the *San Diego Union*, on April 19, Fred Chase, a twelve-year-old newsboy from National City, told his local police that he was selling magazines on the street when a middle-aged man in a dark sedan pulled to the curb and asked him how he could find a vacant shack outside of the city. Chase said that as he was speaking to the driver he saw a girl lying "in the rear of the machine." Chase said the girl, who he thought was Mexican, was crying and her hands were tied.

The *Union* reported that on that same day, twenty-seven-year-old Harold Duncan, a former coworker of Louise who resided at 742 Market Street, was brought to the SDPD Headquarters emergency hospital after patrolmen discovered him wandering blindly through the streets on the east side of town.

They soon learned he had swallowed poison. As he was treated by the police surgeon, Duncan incoherently muttered, "Where is she? Have they found her?"

Duncan told police he was acquainted with Louise and "all of the girls at Kress." After being stabilized, he was sent to the county psych ward for a hold. Five days later, Deputy Sheriff Blake Mason attempted to interview him but discovered that a reporter from the *San Diego Union* had beaten him to the punch.

Duncan told the *Union* he was on a date with a different woman on the night Louise went missing. Duncan provided the names of the young woman and several others who could establish an alibi. When asked if he took poison, Duncan answered, "Yes. I was disappointed with life and couldn't find employment." He added that it was the second time in a year he ingested poison.

The *Union* reporter tracked down Duncan's date. The woman denied seeing Duncan on Saturday but said that on Sunday evening he called her place of employment and the two drove to her East San Diego home. The woman said Duncan stayed there for just a few minutes before leaving. He later took the poison and wound up in the police emergency hospital.

On April 20, Motorcycle Officer Bert Cooper located an abandoned stolen vehicle on El Cajon Avenue and College Way. Inside the car was an overnight bag containing women's underwear and other items. Originally thought to belong to Louise, the bag and items were examined by her grandmother, who said they were not hers.

That same day, Dr. Eldott Colby conducted the postmortem. Because Louise's feet were dragging on the ground and her neck was not broken, the coroner speculated the hanging was a ruse.

Louise was wearing a wristwatch on her left arm, discounting robbery as a motive for her death.

Human skin under the fingernails indicated she fought her attacker. The fight most likely ended with a heavy blow behind her left ear, which knocked her unconscious. Blood clots on the neck indicated Louise was either dead or dying when her attacker put the rope around her neck and lifted her body into the tree.

She had not been sexually assaulted, and a toxicology report indicated she had not been poisoned. Shortly after determining Louise had not committed suicide, authorities had to consider the possibility that she was the victim of a serial killer.

As detectives reviewed the evidence, they noticed that, other than both cases involving females found in semi-remote areas, the cases had significant differences:

1. A person drawn toward killing children most likely would have passed on a victim who looked like an adult.
2. Whoever killed Brooks made a half-hearted effort to hide her. Whoever killed Louise went to the trouble of displaying her.
3. Virginia Brooks was clothed when she was found. Louise Teuber was not.
4. Virginia Brooks had been surgically mutilated. Louise Teuber had not.

According to print media, dozens of possible suspects were looked into, but all were cleared.

On April 21, 1931, R. Harold Newby, a forty-seven-year-old retired navy lieutenant, photographer and Teuber family friend, was questioned for possessing photos of Louise in "an unusual pose." Newby, who resided at 4475 Maryland Avenue, less than a half mile from the Teubers, said he

More than ninety years after Louise Teuber was found, the modest, 860-square-foot, two-bedroom, one-bath Vermont Street Craftsman home is almost completely unchanged from when the family resided in it.

was with his wife in their mountain cabin just outside of Julian on the night Louise died.

His alibi was verified by Mrs. Newby, but he was booked on a charge of possessing illegal photographs. He later posted a $500 bond and was released.

The same day, authorities revealed two notes written by Louise. Both were published by the *San Diego Union*. The first letter, addressed to her father, read: "Dear Dad. I have been trying for a long time to be satisfied with the way you're running the house and I cannot stand it any longer. I am leaving town tonight and not coming back. Louise."

The second note, addressed to her sister Mrs. Isabel Prouty, read: "Sis. When you get this note tell all the folks not to worry. I'm having a good time looking for a job. Awful hot too. I couldn't stay in San Diego another day and I'm going as far as I can. Maybe I'm dippy but try and forget me. Good luck and goodbye. You may hear from me again soon. Louise Teuber." Below her signature was written, "United States of America—Whooopee-e-e-e." Next to the signature she had drawn a cryptograph closely resembling a skull and crossbones.

On April 22, Sheriff Ed Cooper told the press, "We have her activities checked until almost 7 o'clock on Saturday evening and we are confident that between that hour and midnight she met her death."

The Sheriff then went directly after the killer, "The man who did this crime was either very desperate of extremely foolish. He committed the murder in an open glade and selected a spot visible from highway passerby at all times. The oak tree from which her nude body was suspended is the only tree large enough in the vicinity from which he could have hanged her."

According to the April 22 *San Diego Evening Tribune*, a new theory was advanced: Louise may have voluntarily disrobed and was posing for photographs or was an observer and that she was slain somewhere else and then taken to Black Mountain.

The *Tribune* went on to state: "an itinerant commercial photographer, believed to have seen Louise in an automobile after she finished work on Saturday was hunted for questioning. He has been missing for 24 hours and Sheriff Cooper believed the man fled rather than be questioned. Cooper said he thought the man was except the slayer to see Louise alive."

Another theory floated by Sheriff's investigators involved the possibility that Louise was murdered by a woman, a scenario made likely by several scratches to her body made by sharp, pointed fingernails. There also existed the possibility that Louise had not been completely hanged, because the killer was not strong enough to hoist her to a completely vertical position.

On April 23, the city was rocked by news of another slaying. Forty-three-year-old W.B. Bibbens was found brutally murdered in her downtown apartment. For a city that experienced only a dozen homicides in all of 1930, three murders of vulnerable females in less than ninety days was something no one had ever experienced.

The latest murder forced Chief Hill to have the entire bureau focus almost exclusively on the slayings. That decision may have played a part in crime spiking to a five-year high.

Dr. Frank Toomey held the inquest of Louise Teuber on Monday, April 27. A total of seventeen people testified, including one who said Louise "had more male suitors than ten people she knew."

Among the most compelling testimony was that of a woman who said she saw Louise in the passenger seat of a black car on Mission Gorge Road leading out of the city shortly before midnight on April 18. Cattlemen Fred Rickey and Emil Reich recounted seeing a machine turn up the Black Mountain road about 7:00 p.m. on the evening of the eighteenth. The men dismissed it as "probably another petting party."

The area around the long-forgotten Teuber crime scene is now a popular staging area for hikers wishing to climb to the top of 1,593-foot Cowles Mountain, the highest point in the city of San Diego.

Another witness stated that on Sunday morning, April 19, around 1:30 a.m., he drove by the oak grove and observed a black car parked a quarter of a mile from the tree Louise was hanged in.

After being so grief-stricken that he collapsed, William Teuber testified that he and Louise were often at odds. She would attend dances and parties despite being forbidden to leave the house.

The inquest ended without determining the motive for the slaying or who did it.

On April 28, Sheriff Cooper revealed that Louise had told newsboy Morgal Davis that she had a date with a man named Jerry on the night she went missing. Davis went so far as to provide investigators with a license plate of a car Jerry drove, but a check with the California Division of Motor Vehicles found no such plate in existence.

Memorial services were held for Louise on April 29. She was cremated immediately afterward.

After interviewing staff and students at the E.R. Snyder Continuation School, coupled with statements made by the coworkers at Kress, detectives began to theorize that any plans Louise had to relocate were very recent. Detectives surmised that while a secret lover had promised to move Louise from San Diego, in reality, for reasons yet to be determined, they may have been luring her to her death.

On May 1, it was announced that detectives caught up to the secret husband, a marine stationed aboard the USS *West Virginia*. It marked the second time detectives spoke to him about the case. The marine, whose name was withheld, told investigators he knew Louise but that they were not married. The marine said he had been on the ship for the past several weeks and so had not seen her.

The same day, J. Horner, a former sailor and knot-tying instructor, met with detectives and explained that the half splice found on the rope was not a navy knot. Horner added that the rope showed every sign of being used on a block-and-tackle outfit and probably was from a construction or rigging outfit.

On May 9, R. Harold Newby stood in Judge Arthur Mundo's courtroom to be sentenced for taking nude photos of Louise. Newby originally stated that he was a student at the Balboa Park Art School and often did nude portraits. After being charged with violating state obscenity charges and facing years in state prison, he pled guilty in exchange for a lesser sentence.

When he addressed the court, William Teuber expressed shock and dismay that Newby would do such a thing. William said the photos were taken at his daughter's birthday party in the Whispering Pines area just outside the small mountain town of Julian. "I didn't give him permission to take these," William insisted. "She was only 16. I believe these photographs were the cause of my daughters death." William then broke down. Judge Mundo had to call for order several times as the heartbroken father sobbed uncontrollably.

On June 5, the Sheriff's Department announced a reward fund of $1,150 for information in the Teuber case. They still came up empty.

Investigators thought they finally caught a break on October 2, 1931, when a sixteen-year-old sailor named Lowell Milton Bell told Captain William Bright of the Los Angeles County Sheriff's Department that he strangled Louise after she accepted a ride in his car but then refused his advances.

Bell was arrested and sent to San Diego. But while traveling there, he told Undersheriff Oliver Sexson that he only confessed to the murder to get his name on page one of the newspapers. According to reports, Bell told Sexson: "I wanted to become a big town gangster and to go to Chicago and get in a racket. I thought I could if I could work up a reputation, I might get in."

Bell was locked up for his false confession, but his ill-conceived publicity stunt to get on the front pages apparently worked. The story was headlined in newspapers across the United States.

By the end of 1931, several people had come forward to confess to the crime, but none could offer details only the killer or bureau men would know.

On August 15, 1933, Virgil P. Gray, a former Los Angeles County Sheriff's deputy and an expert in forensics, was hired on a $250 per month contract to assist with the investigation. Like those before him, all the clues and evidence led him to a dead end.

In February 1936, Elton Stone, a condemned inmate at San Quentin, was interviewed regarding the Virginia Brooks and Louise Teuber murders. Stone had been sentenced to hang for the killing of fifteen-year-old Mary Louise Stammer of Fresno, California. Deputy Sheriff John Ford conducted the four-hour interview with Stone. In addition to the San Diego cases, Stone was asked about the murder of Bertha Blagg, a Fresno café owner.

Throughout the interview, Stone said: "I have nothing further to admit. I've told you all there is to tell."

A comparison of Stone's fingerprints with the partial print recovered in the Virginia Brooks case did not match. Stone was hanged on June 12, 1936.

Later that month, investigators questioned twenty-six-year-old Leonard Smith of Sacramento after he was arrested for beating two women, one with a hoe and the other with an axe handle. According to Smith, he was stationed in San Diego in 1931 while in the Marine Corps. Smith said that while in San Diego he was arrested on a vagrancy charge. He denied killing Brooks and Teuber.

Detectives later reported being unable to locate an arrest record for anyone matching that name who was attached to the USMC in San Diego in 1931.

5

DIAMOND DOLLY

APRIL 23, 1931.

I t was shortly after 1:00 p.m. when handyman R.B. Brown responded to 1272 Eleventh Street to repair a water pipe inside an apartment. It was his second service call at that address.

On April 17, he knocked on the door of the ground-floor apartment, but no one answered. Figuring no one was home, he returned five days later. This time when no one answered the door, he telephoned the owner, Sam Fox, to meet him.

At first, the men tried to look through a window, but the blinds had been drawn. After pounding on the door and even trying to pry a locked window with no success, they noticed a foul odor emanating from inside. Fox used his pass key to open the door. After peeking inside, he bolted to a telephone to summon the police.

Motorcycle Officer William J. Kennedy was the first officer to respond. After speaking with Fox and Brown, Kennedy entered the apartment, where he discovered the body of thirty-two-year-old Mrs. W.B. Bibbens sprawled across the left side of a bed, clad in a pair of robin-egg-blue silk pajamas. The woman had been battered and slashed. A bloody towel was draped across her face.

Kennedy later described the apartment as "tidy" but said the bedroom was "in shambles having been overhauled by a marauder."

Seeing that the woman had been murdered, the four-year veteran policeman backed out of the apartment and then telephoned headquarters to request homicide bureau men. Captain of Detectives Paul Hayes, along with Detective Lieutenant John Kane and Detective Sergeant Harry Leech, responded. The trio was joined by Deputy Coroner Dave Gershon.

The investigators ascertained that Bibbens, known to her friends as "Diamond Dolly" because of her affection for the carbon-based stone, was a horse-racing fan and spent time at local tracks. She was last seen on Wednesday, April 15, when she paid rent to Lois Parker, the property manager who resided at 1027 A Street (within sight of the crime scene).

Parker told Captain Hayes that Bibbens leased the apartment on November 10, 1930, with a man assumed to be her husband. Parker added that Bibbens was an excellent tenant and caused no trouble.

A door-to-door check for witnesses located several neighbors who said they believed the husband to be "a traveling man" and said they had seen little of him since Diamond Dolly moved in.

Police ultimately discovered that Bibbens was a widow; her husband committed suicide in Los Angeles in September 1930. The man who rented the apartment with her was Walter W. Bartleman, an elevator operator. He was eventually cleared as a suspect.

A 1934 *New York Daily News* article on the series of murders reported that Bibbens's vehicle was missing at the time her body was discovered and was never recovered.

A methodical search of the usually tidy apartment revealed moldy food in the kitchen. One anomaly was a fresh bowl of bananas. The detectives also found two dead goldfish in a fish tank in the living room. Assuming that the fish had starved, coupled with the condition of the body and the latest newspaper dated April 16, investigators surmised that Bibbens had been dead approximately one week.

In the bedroom, investigators noted that a trunk containing personal items had been ransacked, as if the killer was looking for something specific. Detectives noted that in addition to a small gold woman's watch left in plain view on the dresser, Bibbens was wearing a small diamond ring and a guard ring on her right hand. On another finger on her right hand the skin had been torn, as if a ring had been ripped off.

Detectives also recovered a woman's smock inside the apartment. In one of the pockets was a handkerchief with the initials "H.C."

Detectives noted that while the apartment had been rented to a couple, there were only two pairs of men's pants inside. There were no male shirts, neckties, hair products or grooming items anywhere to be found.

Dr. Frank Toomey conducted the autopsy. He listed the cause of death as strangulation. Toomey also located several small, sandy-colored hairs under Bibbens' fingernails, possibly from a mustache.

With Virginia Brooks and Louise Teuber still in the headlines, panic spread across the city. Due diligence demanded that detectives consider whether the Bibbens killing was the work of the person or persons who killed Brooks and Teuber.

Other than all three victims being female, the cases couldn't have been more different. All three were of different ages, demographics and social circles. The one commonality was the method of death. All three had been strangled. But strangulation is a common method of killing for an unarmed assailant.

Even the strangulation methods were not the same. Brooks was strangled with a garrot. Evidence indicated that Teuber and Bibbens were most likely strangled with bare hands.

On Thursday, April 30, 1931, the police department announced that thirty-seven-year-old Henry Charles "H.C." Yardley, a former cook on a San Diego–based fishing boat, had been arrested for the Bibbens murder in Uniontown, Pennsylvania, shortly after stepping off a train. Captain Hayes told the *San Diego Union*, "We've woven a set of circumstances around Yardley's connection with the slaying that implicates him deeply."

Among the incriminating circumstances was that Yardley had been seen with Bibbens as late as April 15.

Laundry marks on the male's pants recovered from inside the apartment led detectives to W.B. Vignault, a laundry driver who served both Yardley and Mrs. Bibbens. Vignault said that about a month earlier, Yardley had stolen blankets and sixty-seven dollars from a trunk inside Bibbens' apartment. According to Vignault, Yardley had threatened Bibbens when they confronted him and demanded he return the blankets and repay the money.

Days before the murder, Yardley had been spotted at a Market Street rooming house with two men from Detroit, Peter Moore and a man known only as "Miller." Listing his address as 1272 Eleventh Street, Yardley told the rooming house landlady that he would "stand good for their bill."

Detectives learned that Moore and Miller stiffed the landlady when they, along with Yardley, left San Diego abruptly on April 16 around 1:00 a.m. As Yardley traveled toward the East Coast, he stopped in St. Louis, where he pawned a handbag that belonged to Bibbens for $3.50.

California governor James C. Rolph approved extraditing Yardley back to San Diego, and Yardley was locked in the County Jail pending an April 18, 1931 preliminary hearing. When detectives interviewed Yardley in the San Diego jail, he denied killing Bibbens. When asked about the handbag, he insisted it had been given to him by the murdered woman as a "gift of affection."

On June 17, Yardley's attorney, J.H. McKinney, filed a motion to dismiss the charge due to insufficient evidence, primarily, that an exact time of death could not be established.

The preliminary hearing was held on June 18, with Deputy District Attorney Sam Bristow representing the people. W.B. Vignault testified to the laundry marks. When Bristow showed Vignault the bag that had been pawned in St. Louis, Vignault positively identified it as the one he had seen Bibben with.

McKinney objected. Arguing that the bag was not so unique that it could be the only one in existence, Justice Eugene Dany Jr. struck the bag from being admitted as evidence.

Earl Campbell, an iceman, testified that he made a delivery to Bibbens's apartment on the fifteenth and "even passed some time of day" with Yardley until being paid fifteen cents for the ice. Campbell then went on his way.

Newsboy William Koler testified that he delivered the newspaper to Bibbens's door on the sixteenth and that later it was gone.

McKinney argued that since Yardley left San Diego at 1:00 a.m. on the sixteenth, he wasn't there to take the newspaper inside the apartment. McKinney then picked apart a report from Detective Sergeant Harry Leech in which he mentioned the bowl of bananas being fresher than he would have accepted if they were a week old.

Doctor Toomey testified that Bibbens died of strangulation and that her death might have occurred "four or five days or it might have been a week" before her body was found.

The hearing ended with Justice Eugene Dany Jr. approving the defense motion and dismissing the charge. Yardley was ordered released, and the murder charge was dropped. After learning that the murder charge had been dismissed, Detective Captain Jasper "Jack" Berg ordered Detective Lieutenant Harry Kelly to begin a "careful study of the entire case."

Berg then told the press, "Yardley is not entirely eliminated. If we can secure enough evidence to implicate him in the case we may ask for a new

The San Diego County Jail, then located at Union and C Streets, held some of the area's most notorious criminals, including Henry Charles "H.C." Yardley, as they awaited trial. Unfortunately, the jail would be the last place to hold Yardley after the DA's case fell apart in court. *Courtesy of San Diego Police Museum.*

complaint." Berg added that the police department was looking for the two men who left town with Yardley to question them about the killing.

Two days after the criminal case was dismissed, all of Dolly Bibbens's possessions were auctioned after no living heirs to her estate could be located. The sale was held in the same apartment where she met her violent end. According to the *New York Daily News*, "hundreds of curiosity seekers jammed the flat."

The Bibbens case went cold until March 1934, when a fifty-two-year-old horse trainer named John E. Davis was arrested in New Orleans. According to the New Orleans Police Department, Davis was known to visit the racetrack and admitted he knew Diamond Dolly. Davis also admitted to being in San Diego when the murder occurred but insisted he didn't do it.

The New Orleans police reported that Davis had clippings about the murder in his possession as well as a pawn slip from a shop located at 802 Fifth Avenue in San Diego. According to the slip, Davis pawned a stickpin that belonged to Bibbens on March 4, 1931.

The 1889 San Diego Courthouse at 220 West Broadway hosted some of San Diego's most sensational trials prior to its 1959 demolition. The Italianate-style building included a bell and clock tower, a ten-foot gilded statue of Justice and forty-two stained-glass windows honoring each state. Today, the old windows are displayed in the walkways of the Hall of Justice at 333 West Broadway. *Courtesy of San Diego Police Museum.*

If the news looked promising, it didn't last. On March 12, Detective Lieutenant Kane instructed police in New Orleans to release Davis. After reviewing all of the evidence in the case, it was determined that Davis was not connected to the slaying.

6

THE INDIAN VILLAGE MURDERER

MAY 3, 1931.

I t was shortly after noon when two young Cub Scouts, nine-year-old Richard Roehl of 4050 Park Boulevard and his neighbor, ten-year-old Jess Zimmerman of 4034 Park Boulevard, found the body of twenty-three-year-old Hazel Bradshaw secreted in a patch of hare barley weeds in the Indian Village section of Balboa Park. The scene was less than 150 yards from where Detective Charles Harris was murdered in the line of duty in 1927.

The petite woman was lying on her back, fully clothed in an open, light silk topcoat. Her smart, cream-colored frock was slashed to ribbons and soaked with blood. Her hat was crumpled under her head, and her petite wristwatch, attached to her left arm, had stopped at 9:43. Just below the watchband were wound marks. Despite her dress being pulled above her waist, she had not been sexually assaulted.

Deputy Coroner Dave Gershon later took the watch and shook it. The timepiece ran for another four hours.

The savagery of the attack indicated the killer was motivated by a personal rage. Of seventeen stab wounds, nine would have been fatal. The depth of the wounds indicated that a large blade, probably a butcher knife, was the murder weapon. The knife was never found for a positive match.

Five feet from the body was a larger pool of blood, indicating Hazel may have attempted to crawl away from her assailant.

A milk bottle containing a small amount of liquid, possibly wine, was found not far from her body.

Detectives noted that the body was discovered behind a wall that surrounded Indian Village. In order to get behind the wall without going through the main entrance on the west side of the village (abutting the Boy Scout camp), a person would need to crawl through a relatively small hole in a wire fence.

Had she not been willing to accompany someone through the fence, it would have been almost impossible for an assailant to drag her through if she was resisting.

Within an hour of the discovery, the entire SDPD Detective Bureau had been notified. Captain of Detectives Paul Hayes took charge of the investigation.

Hazel lived at 4510 Alabama Street, approximately 1.6 miles north of where her body was discovered. She worked as a telephone operator at a

Detective points to spot where body of Hazel Bradshaw, attractive young telephone operator, was found. Scene was the Indian village built for the Panama-Pacific Exposition and later turned over to the Boy Scouts. The body bore seventeen knife wounds.

A reporter photographed the squad of detectives at the scene of the Bradshaw murder. To their right is the wall and sidewalk that Moss Garrison admitted to walking on the night of the slaying.

Creepy Moss E. Garrison became a top suspect from the moment he walked into police headquarters. That opinion only intensified as detectives began looking into his past.

local railway company. Along with her sister Mildred, she was the sole support for a family of nine children.

Hazel's murder was the second tragedy to befall the family in the previous few months. Her older brother Frank, a Pensacola-based sailor, had been an innocent bystander when he was shot and killed the previous December. The morticians who handled Frank Bradshaw's body were the same ones assigned to Hazel.

As the city struggled with news of another vicious slaying, the May 4, 1931 *San Diego Union* ran the headline, "Girl, 19, Victim in Chain of Murders," implying a serial killer was at work across the city.

Detectives learned Hazel was involved in a romantic relationship with thirty-eight-year-old Moss E. Garrison, a coworker who worked in the railroad commissary.

According to those who knew, Hazel also had the eye of a U.S. Navy Chief Warrant Officer named Harry Glixton. According to media reports, hours after news of the murder broke, Glixton came to Police Headquarters saying he read about the killing in the newspaper. He was questioned and, after establishing a solid alibi, released.

As detectives were discussing where to find Garrison, he walked into Police Headquarters. He said he also learned of the murder in the newspaper and wanted to help find the killer. He voluntarily agreed to be interviewed by Chief Arthur Hill and Captain Hayes.

In his statement, Garrison said he took Hazel to two shows downtown, the last being at the Superba Theatre at 301 C Street. They then left the theatre at 10:55 p.m. and walked north on Fifth Avenue. On reaching Laurel Street, Garrison said the couple walked east, across the Cabrillo Bridge and then through Balboa Park. When they reached Park Boulevard, the couple walked north to 4510 Alabama Street.

Despite conceding that the walk took them within a few feet of where Hazel was found, Garrison denied killing her. He claimed when they arrived at the Bradshaw home at 11:55 p.m., the family car was parked in front as usual.

Garrison insisted he last saw Hazel when he walked her to the front door and kissed her goodnight. The last thing Hazel said was, "Hurry or you'll miss your car," meaning the streetcar. After hearing the screen door slam, Garrison said he walked one mile south to University Avenue, where he caught the number 11 streetcar at the Park Junction stop located at Park Boulevard and University.

As he was being questioned, Captain Hayes noticed two small cuts on Garrison's right index finger. "What happened?" Hayes asked.

"I cut my finger using the automatic bread slicer at work."

Lloyd Meirs of the Identification Bureau photographed the injury. Police Surgeon Paul Brust, MD, examined the wound and then bandaged it. In his case notes, Dr. Brust noted that Garrison's trousers had bloodstains on the fringes of where the pockets had been torn out.

"What happened to your pants?" the doctor inquired. Garrison responded that he tore out his pockets to use as a bandage for his cut finger.

The San Diego streetcar system was decommissioned in 1947. Most of the rails were paved over and the cars either sold off, sent to museums or left to the elements. Streetcar 138 now resides at the National City Railroad Museum and is the same type that Moss Garrison took on the night of the killing. *Courtesy Neil Joseph.*

Dr. Brust also noted that several small pieces of barley weed were trapped in the cuff of Garrison's trousers.

If Chief Hill and Captain Hayes had a hard time believing their ears with Garrison's story, they could hardly believe their eyes when they accompanied him to the morgue to view Hazel's body. Not only did he not demonstrate shock or horror on seeing his girlfriend's mutilated corpse, he also kissed the girl's forehead and exclaimed, "Ah, little sweetheart, little sweetheart!"

By now, detectives had enough probable cause to hold Garrison. As Hill and Hayes booked him on a charge of murder, Detective Sergeant Fred Lightner met with Hazel's family. Both her father, C.A. Bradshaw, and mother, Cora, confirmed that Hazel frequently went downtown on Saturday nights for the theater, but they took issue with Garrison's statement that she had come home.

According to both parents, Garrison always came into the house after a date with their daughter.

Insisting Hazel never came home, Mr. Bradshaw said he and Cora had been up until after 11:00 p.m. He said he was still awake past midnight and that his bedroom was fifteen feet from the front door. Mr. Bradshaw insisted the screen door never slammed, as he and his wife would have heard it. Bradshaw added that Bozo, the small family dog, who barked at anyone coming into the house, family or not, never made a sound.

Sergeant Lightner noted that Hazel's bed had not been touched.

Garrison's story of "catching the number 11" was verified by J.M. Hughes, the motorman who was operating the San Diego Electric Railway Pullman Standard streetcar that night. Hughes said he knew Garrison on sight, as he rode the streetcar nearly every Saturday night. He said Garrison got onto the tram at about twelves minutes past midnight. According to Hughes, Garrison didn't seem agitated and didn't act as if anything was out of the ordinary.

But Hughes couldn't attest where Garrison had come from. The Park Boulevard and University Avenue stop was one mile south of Hazel's home and six-tenths of a mile north of where her body was discovered.

Sergeant Lightner noted that the Park and University streetcar stop would not have been the first one Garrison encountered if he had been walking south from Alabama Street. He could have caught the same streetcar nine blocks closer at Park and El Cajon Boulevard.

There was also the issue of why the couple walked more than a mile and a half from the downtown theater at all. The number 1 streetcar picked up at

Fifth Avenue and C Street and proceeded north to University Avenue, where it turned right and became the number 11.

While meeting with the family, Cora Bradshaw told Sergeant Lightner of a letter Garrison had sent to Hazel a few weeks earlier. "'I want you to see what mushy letters this fellow Garrison writes to me,'" Cora said Hazel told her. "She had the open letter in her hand. Then Hazel said: 'Oh that man Garrison! He worries me to death. He's the type that would kill a girl.'"

Cora said, "When I told Hazel that I'd been worrying about her and that I was afraid someone would kill her she said 'well, I have been threatened.'"

Sergeant Lightner's reports mention that Hazel's father and sisters Edith and Bobbie, as well as her seventeen-year-old brother Omer, all said that on various occasions she had been threatened by Garrison.

When Lightner asked the family where their car was parked on the night Hazel went missing, Omer said, "I parked the car inside early [around 7:30 p.m.] as no one was using it."

In any domestic relationship in which one person winds up murdered, the other person in the relationship is a logical suspect. But detectives learned of a prior love interest, a sailor named U.S. Wilson. Stationed aboard the battleship USS *California*, Wilson may have had a motive. He needed to be looked at.

According to Cora, an unknown male telephoned Hazel on Friday evening and said, "If I can't have you no one else can. I'll kill you then I'll kill myself."

Substantiating the jealous lover theory was Walter Ham, a neighbor who frequently gave Hazel rides to work and back home. According to Ham, he overhead Hazel on the phone on Friday around 5:30 p.m. telling an unknown caller, "It's over."

Sergeant Lightner located U.S. Wilson, who said he had known Hazel from his time in Washington State. They renewed their relationship when he came to live in San Diego. Wilson added that the couple had been engaged until Christmas 1929.

Wilson told Sergeant Lightner that he was visiting Hazel in December 1930 when there was a knock at the door. "I went to the door," Wilson said. "I saw a man who was backing away. I heard him say 'I'll go back and get my gun and shoot both of you.' Later I made Hazel tell me his name. She said it was Moss Garrison."

"Did she tell you of previous threats?"

"She told me many times how she feared him. She said he had proposed marriage and she felt he would kill her if she didn't accept."

As detectives reviewed evidence, including information that Garrison had once been involved in a shooting in Savannah, Georgia, in which three men were wounded, Motorcycle Officer Clarence E. Renner volunteered to walk the route Garrison claimed the couple took on the night of the slaying. Saying he walked rapidly, Renner timed himself at fifty-six minutes, thirty-five seconds.

Renner wasn't the only one who found the timing curious. Newspaperman Tod Bates also paced off the distance, in one hour, twenty-four minutes. The second time, Bates was joined by his wife, and the pair completed the route in one hour, ten minutes.

On May 7, 1931, Captain Hayes told the press that police had recovered a bloody necktie inside Garrison's apartment. Hayes said he took the tie to the jail, where he confronted Garrison. According to the case notes, Captain Hayes held the necktie in front of Garrison and demanded, "Is this the tie you wore last Saturday night?"

"No," Garrison replied.

"Is it one of your ties?" Hayes fired back.

Garrison then admitted the tie belonged to him but remained steadfast that he did not have it on during the night Hazel was murdered.

Hayes provided the tie to Walter Macy, who determined that it contained blood. Limits of forensic science at the time could not positively match it to Hazel Bradshaw.

On Monday, May 11, Deputy Coroner Dave Gershon began the inquest before a nine-man, one-woman jury. Moss Garrison, his brother C.A. Garrison and attorney Abijah Fairchild also attended.

The *San Diego Union* reported that Garrison Moss appeared at the inquest clean-shaven and looking rested. The newspaper stated that Moss reportedly appeared "keenly interested" and at times a faint smile crossed his face as Gershon presented the evidence, specifically when SDPD Identification Tech Lloyd Meirs presented photographs of the crime scene and body.

According to reports, Hayes later visited Garrison in his jail cell. "You go to bed early don't you?"

"Yes. I was reading and I fell asleep," Garrison answered.

"Did you dream about your sweetheart?"

"No I didn't."

"Well Garrison," the lumbering six-foot, six-inch captain said, "a fellow who loved a girl like you loved Hazel Bradshaw certainly ought to dream about her: her curly hair, her sparkling blue eyes and winning smile which everyone loved. Did they make you dream of her?"

"No sir."

Hayes pressed on by describing the blood-saturated crime scene. "Doesn't that make you think of her?"

"No sir," Garrison replied.

At the June 1, 1931 preliminary hearing, Edith Bradshaw testified that she and Hazel often fought about other men with Garrison. Adding that she often attended the theater with her sister and Garrison, Edith said that on one occasion the couple was in such a heated argument that she and Hazel ran away in fear. Edith said Garrison caught up to them and then slammed their heads together.

The defense conceded that Garrison was with Hazel on the night of the slaying but presented a theory: after Garrison walked her home, she left the house and went back to Balboa Park, where she met the real killer.

At one point during the two-day hearing, C.A. Garrison was admonished for carrying a concealed handgun into the courtroom. After producing a concealed weapons permit, C.A. was informed that only a peace officer could carry a gun into a courtroom. He was told to lock the gun in his safe at home or face arrest.

The hearing ended with Garrison bound over to face trial for murder. The trial opened in the last week of July 1931.

One of the witnesses was Louis Lechien, who testified that he saw Garrison and a girl on Seventh Street between Broadway and C on the night of May 2 at around 8:25 or 8:30 p.m. He said Hazel and Garrison were walking toward Broadway and that Garrison was showing his companion something he had in a box he was carrying.

Lechien was the first witness to back up Garrison's statement that he was downtown with Hazel on the night she was killed. What Lechien couldn't answer was what Garrison was wearing. When cross-examined by defense attorney Abijah Fairchild, Lechien admitted he was more interested in the man's companion than in him.

"Isn't it true that your wife wanted you to come along and stop looking at the girl?" Fairchild asked.

"Yes sir."

Mr. and Mrs. George Letson testified that between 11:45 p.m. and midnight they were sitting in their car near the north end of Indian Village when they saw a figure pass within a few feet of them headed north. Mr. Letson said he wasn't sure if the figure was male or female.

Mrs. Letson was more specific. She said the figure was a male of less than medium build, and she judged him to be between thirty-five and forty years old.

Evelyn Myers of 3976 Arizona Street testified that at around 11:40 p.m. she and her husband, along with another couple, were driving north on Park Boulevard, passing Indian Village, when she heard a woman scream. Myers described it as a "sweet voice in distress."

Myers admitted that no one else in the car heard the screams.

During cross-examination by Fairchild, the defense attorney tried to get Myers to admit the sound could have been that of a zoo animal emanating from the large wildlife refuge less than two hundred yards west of Indian Village.

"I'm certain it was a woman screaming," Myers insisted.

"When did you learn about the murder?" Fairchild asked.

"The next day."

"And you didn't tell the police what you heard?" Fairchild pressed.

"No."

W.H. Parker, an employee of the railroad, testified to the finger cut Dr. Brust had examined. Parker said Garrison had access to knives as part of his duties but that the railroad did not own an automatic bread slicer.

On the afternoon of July 22, 1931, Captain Paul Hayes was being cross-examined by Fairchild when things became testy. When asked about the exact time the Bradshaw family car was parked in front of the home, Captain Hayes said, "I don't know."

"You don't know much do you?" Fairchild fired back.

Judge Lawrence N. Turrentine interrupted Fairchild, forcing the defense attorney to beg for the court's pardon. "He provokes me," Fairchild explained. "He could answer my questions if he would."

Earlier, Hayes had responded several times to Fairchild's questions with, "I'm not answering hearsay." Judge Turrentine instructed the captain to simply respond no if he didn't know the answer to further questions.

Fairchild then pressed Hayes as to how he responded to Garrison's request for an attorney. "Did you not tell Garrison 'to hell with his attorney, that you were the law'?"

"I told him you have no jurisdiction over me."

"You tried to give the defendant an injection didn't you?" the defense attorney demanded. He was referring to truth serum, a colloquial name for a range of psychoactive drugs used to obtain information from subjects who are unable or unwilling to provide it otherwise

"No I did not," Hayes responded. "I asked him if he'd take an injection. He said 'no' that he didn't want it. I then asked him what if the doctor thought he needed it."

Garrison later said he was not injected.

"Did you tell Garrison that if he would plead guilty you would see to it that he was not hanged?"

"No."

Fairchild shifted. "Have there not been three other murders in and around San Diego prior to the Bradshaw murder?"

Hayes paused.

"You don't care to answer that do you?" Fairchild demanded.

"Your question is not proper," Judge Turrentine interrupted.

"Well things were getting desperate in San Diego and you were vigorous to solve a murder weren't you Captain?"

"No more than any other murder," Hayes responded.

"You tried to get results? You were pressed?"

"No."

Questioning then turned to the pieces of hare barley weed found in the cuff of Garrison's pants. Fairchild got Hayes to concede it was very common to get the weed stuck in trouser cuffs.

In closing arguments of the one-week trial, Deputy District Attorney Oran Muir told the jury that the killing was the most "beastly crime he had seen in his twenty years of practicing law." He then walked the jury through the evidence, Garrison's jealousy and the timeline of events. He summarized the case by saying, "If the defendant did not kill her then it is most remarkable that her body should be found where Garrison himself admitted to being."

Muir then implored the jury to use logic. "Did Hazel Bradshaw ever reach home that night? If she did the defendant didn't kill her. But if she did not then the defendant is guilty. When you find him guilty you have only done half your duty" Muir added. "I have never asked a jury to do something I wouldn't do myself and I ask you now, by your verdict, to sentence the defendant to hang by the neck until he is dead."

In his closing arguments, Abijah Fairchild chose to put the police department, specifically Paul Hayes, on trial. "This is the first time in my twenty five years of experience as an attorney that I've seen a defendant called upon to prove himself innocent instead of the prosecution being called on to prove him guilty," Fairchild told the jury.

After reminding the jurors the police could not produce an eyewitness to the slaying, Fairchild suggested that Hazel left home after she parted ways with Garrison and returned to the park for a party that his client knew nothing about.

"Not one man killed that girl," Fairchild insisted. "No one man could have dragged her body through that hole in the fence or thrown her body over the wall."

Fairchild ended his remarks by saying, "When you've given every bit of evidence in this case your attention, you'll bring back a verdict of not guilty.

The jurors took the case on Friday, July 30. They deliberated just ninety minutes before acquitting Garrison Moss of murder. At 4:30 p.m., he walked out of jail a free man.

It didn't take long for him to resurface in the San Diego jail, however. He was arrested on September 15, 1931, by Officer Byron Hamond during a downtown sweep of illegal gambling sites.

The murder case of Hazel Bradshaw is officially listed as unsolved.

Garrison Moss died in Miami, Florida, in September 1966.

7

A MOST UNLIKELY SUSPECT

JUNE 13, 1933.

Claude Trader began his workday as part of a four-man crew painting the Giant Dipper wooden roller coaster at Mission Beach. Around 1:00 p.m., the thirty-four-year-old licensed painting contractor was interrupted by a stranger wearing a light-green sweater-vest.

According to coworkers, Trader met the man on the sidewalk next to the towering coaster and spoke to him. Around 1:15 p.m., the men left in their personal vehicles, one following the other.

Shortly after 1:30 p.m., the pair wound up at 4026 Boundary Street, where Trader shared the tidy, one-thousand-square-foot, two-bedroom clapboard house with his mother, Blanche.

According to the *San Diego Union*, Blanche said the stranger waited in his car while her son went into the house to get a tape measure, a tablet and two pencils. Claude told his mother, "I'm going to Escondido to figure on a job. I'll be back about 5 o'clock. Have the bathwater ready because I'm going out tonight." Blanche then watched as her son got into the passenger side of the stranger's vehicle and they drove north toward Escondido.

According to statements made to Detective Ed Dieckmann, eighteen-year-old Raymond Parker said he was walking along Ward Road at the northern city limits of Mission Valley when Claude and his friend pulled to the side of the road and offered him a ride.

Raymond said that after getting into the car, the men drove the Murray Canyon inland highway to the southern outskirts of Escondido when the

The iconic Giant Dipper roller coaster at Mission Beach played an important part in the timeline of the disappearance and murder of Claude Trader. *Courtesy of San Diego Police Museum.*

stranger stopped and told Raymond, "This is as far as we're going; you can get out here."

According to the police report, Raymond looked at Claude and asked, "Where are you going?"

"I'm going to figure on a paint job," Claude responded. He then turned to the stranger and asked, "Isn't that right?" The stranger nodded.

Raymond told Detective Dieckmann he last saw the men when the car then turned off the highway and headed southeast on a dirt road toward San Pasqual.

When her son did not return home that evening, Blanche filed a missing person report with both the San Diego Police Department and the San Diego County Sheriff. In her report, Blanche told officers that at around 10:00 a.m. on the day Claude went missing, a caller named "McGinness" telephoned the house saying he wanted to speak with Claude about work. She also listed others who might know of her son's whereabouts, including a hospital nurse named Hazel Blanc and a mutual friend of Blanc's and her son's, a married San Diego police officer named Gerhard A. Cordes.

When detectives spoke to Hazel, they learned that she was supposed have a date with Trader on the evening he went missing. They also learned that

Cordes had expressed a romantic interest in her but that the feelings were not mutual. When detectives spoke to Cordes, he denied knowing Trader.

The vast majority of cases result in the missing person turning up, often voluntarily. But there were no signs of Trader. Within a week, the case had grown from a routine missing person situation to a statewide search.

On June 22, 1933, Trader's body was recovered in a patch of wild grapevines along a desolate dirt road in the San Pasqual Valley. The location was just south of the Escondido town limits and approximately thirty-three miles north of his home.

Forrest Rennick, a friend of Trader who had taken it upon himself to search for his friend, made the discovery and telephoned the Sheriff. Deputy Sheriff Herbert Kennedy responded. In his subsequent report, Kennedy noted that the evidence suggested Trader was killed in the same spot where the body was located.

Kennedy later told the press, "From what we found at the scene Trader was apparently shot without the slightest warning by the mysterious stranger. The stranger apparently stopped the automobile beside the vines which almost covered the roadway, and as Trader stepped out of the machine, fired one shot."

"That shot," Kennedy said, "struck Trader in the head and I believe the slayer even may have caught the body and let it fall in the heavy under growth about five or six feet from the side of the road. The wild grape vine grew over the body within the last few days. I don't believe Trader had an opportunity to fight for his life."

Despite an exhaustive search, the murder weapon was not located.

During the time Trader was missing, Blanche reported to police that the mysterious Mr. McGinness had called two more times asking for her son.

Dr. Frank Toomey conducted the postmortem. The advanced state of decomposition indicated that Trader was most likely killed the day he vanished. According to Toomey's report, Trader had been shot once in the right temple.

After being removed from Trader's head, the bullet was sent to Los Angeles for a forensic ballistics examination.

On June 17, Detective Lieutenant Joe Doran and Detective Sergeant Ed Dieckmann met with Raymond Parker at the Linda Vista airport, where Trader kept a plane.

Raymond told the investigators that the mystery car was a 1929 Chrysler coupe with wire wheels. The driver was a white male, thirty-five to forty years old, with dark hair and a dark complexion with "muscles showing through his skin." Raymond said the mystery man was wearing a blue coat, a white shirt with a black necktie and brown pants.

Cordes stood six feet, one inch tall with a slender build and fit the general description except for lighter-colored hair. But when shown a photo of the policeman, Parker couldn't positively identify him as the driver.

SDPD Identification Bureau personnel checked motor vehicle records for all 1929 Chryslers and Plymouths in San Diego County. Of 474 cars found, they discovered Gerhard Cordes owned a 1929 black Plymouth coupe. In a related report filed by Detective Charles Padget, he stated, "it is easy to confuse a 1929 Chrysler with a 1929 Plymouth. Except for a one inch difference in length, the cars are identical."

By now, rumors were spreading across the city that a San Diego policeman could be responsible for Claude Trader going missing.

On July 9, a reporter interviewed Cordes. His statements appeared in the July 10 *San Diego Union*. Cordes said: "I've never so much as met Trader and I certainly don't know him. Since Trader's death a friend of mine recalled an incident at 5th and University Avenues and I was reminded that a man I had seen halt his car and wait for traffic signals to change was Trader."

Cordes continued, "On the night before Trader disappeared I was driving a police radio patrol car. I went to work at 8:45 p.m. and worked until 3 o'clock the next morning. Upon leaving work I went home and slept until about 12:30 p.m. After getting up and having my breakfast, although it was after noon, I went for a drive in my car. I didn't leave the city. As I recall I went to Balboa Park and parked my machine where I could look down [from the mesa] over the city. I also drove down by the waterfront."

Cordes told the *San Diego Union* that afterward he went to a drive-in sandwich stand at Seventh and University Avenue around 3:00 p.m., then later to another drive-in sandwich stand at Park Boulevard and Russ Street near San Diego High. He said he returned home by 5:00 p.m. and reported for duty at the Central Station that night.

On July 11, Undersheriff Oliver Sexston told the *San Diego Union* that the Trader murder was solved but that there was not enough evidence to convict the unnamed suspect.

On July 12, Sheriff's Detectives recruited a diver to search Lake Hodges, under the inland highway bridge, for the murder weapon. Nothing was found.

On July 14, Sheriff's Detectives received a tip that Claude Trader had recently purchased a revolver and was being threatened for his affections toward a woman. When detectives went to ask Blanche about the threats, they discovered her with relatives "in a state of collapse" and unable to be questioned.

By July 27, SDPD Detectives and their sheriff counterparts had compiled enough circumstantial evidence against Cordes that Chief of Police John T. Peterson took the patrolman's badge and gun and suspended him without pay.

Not coincidently, that same day, Sheriff Edgar Cooper's office delivered a criminal case to the DA requesting murder charges against Cordes. After reviewing the case, District Attorney Thomas Whelan told the Sheriff he needed additional evidence if charges were to be filed.

A Grand Jury was convened in the last week of July. Among the witnesses to testify was Los Angeles ballistics expert Frank Gompertz, who stated that the bullet that killed Trader was a reload fired from a Colt Special .38-caliber revolver similar to those used by SDPD officers. Gompertz was careful to point out that members of the public also had reloaded ammo.

Officer Alfred Schnepp then testified that he returned from vacation to discover his duty weapon, a Colt .38-caliber revolver, missing from his locker inside Police Headquarters. Schnepp, the prowl car partner of Cordes, filed a police report and was issued a new gun.

After hearing from more than a score of witnesses, on July 29, the Grand Jury indicted Gerhard Cordes for murder.

According to the *San Diego Union*, SDPD Detectives arrested Cordes at his home moments after the indictment was revealed and delivered him to Judge Lloyd Griffin. The *Union* said Cordes calmly stood wearing a light-green sweater-vest and chewing gum as he listened to the judge read the indictment.

On August 16, Cordes formally pled not guilty to the charge of murder. Judge Griffin set bail at $10,000. Judge Arthur Mundo later reduced the bail to $3,000, and on August 23, Cordes posted bond and was released. He remained free until his September 6 trial.

The six-day trial began at 10:00 a.m., with Judge Mundo presiding. Gordon Thompson, Chief Deputy District Attorney, and Deputy District Attorney Oran Muir represented the people of the State of California. For the defense was attorney Edgar B. Hervey.

As a "record breaking crowd" of mostly female spectators packed the Victorian-era courtroom, Muir told the six-man, six-woman jury that the state would present a case of jealousy that led to murder and introduce circumstantial evidence against Cordes that would prove his guilt beyond a reasonable doubt.

Officer Alfred Schnepp. Had his stolen gun been located shortly after the Trader murder, ballistics could have tied it directly to Gerhard Cordes. *Courtesy of San Diego Police Museum.*

Hervey had a different take. "The defense believes we can show you more about this case than can the Sheriff's Office."

The first witness was Dr. Toomey, who testified to the condition of the body and removing the bullet.

He was followed by Forest Rennick, a former federal investigator in the Foreign Service with extensive investigation experience. Rennick said he had been searching Trader since June 15 and finally located him after detecting an odor near the road. "I found the body about seven feet off the highway," Rennick testified. "The feet were nearest the road with the body extending down a steep embankment. Where the body was found was not wide enough for a machine to turn around without being jockeyed several times."

Rennick said that, considering where the body was found, it would have been visible only from the ranch house of Reginald H. McGinness, which sat approximately half a mile away.

Sheriff Cooper later testified that the rancher was the victim of a plot. "R.H. McGinness in no way answers the description of the stranger who drove the coupe and we are satisfied with his movements that day," the Sheriff declared. "But the man who killed Trader had to know something of McGinness to use the name and a logical story that led him to his death."

During the trial, Blanche Trader testified that she recognized the voice of McGinness as that of Cordes. On cross-examination, however, she admitted that she could have been mistaken.

Deputy Sheriff Wayne Macy testified that on June 27 he paced the drive from the Giant Dipper to 4026 Boundary Street. Driving at speeds between twenty-five and forty-seven miles per hour, he then drove from Boundary Street to Ward Road, then to San Pasqual. He eventually wound up at Seventh and University. Macy said it took from 1:15 p.m. to 3:23 p.m.

Fern Hawkes worked as a waitress at Glenn's Drive-In at Seventh Avenue and University. She told the jury that on Tuesday, June 13, Cordes came in and ordered beer. Hawkes said Cordes returned the following Saturday around noon, asking her to recall when he was last there sampling beer. Hawkes said that Cordes told her, "There's a man missing and the authorities are trying to say I bumped him off."

Hawkes said she checked her sales slips and noted that she had served Cordes at 3:00 p.m. She recalled Cordes as wearing a brown suit and driving a black Plymouth coupe when she saw him on Tuesday. She added, "When I talked with Cordes on Saturday after he had been in on Tuesday, and later when he knew I testified before the Grand Jury, he always told me to tell the truth, whether it was for or against him."

Several times, Chief District Attorney Thompson pressed Hawkes to admit that the June 13 encounter was closer to 3:30 p.m., but her testimony never wavered.

Lee Thomas, a waitress at a Twelfth Avenue and A Street sandwich shop, also took the stand. She testified that Cordes was at the shop at 4:15 p.m. wanting to sample a new beer. Thomas said Cordes was wearing a white shirt, a black necktie and brown pants. She saw a blue coat rolled up on the front seat and mentioned that it could get wrinkled. Cordes told her not to worry about it. Thomas said she also saw a revolver in the car but knew Cordes was a policeman.

Thomas said she remembered the time because she told Cordes that a city ordinance prohibited her from selling beer before 4:30 due to the shop's proximity to Russ (San Diego High) School across the street.

On September 10, twenty-year-old Hazel Blanc, whom the press described as "comely," testified that she met Claude Trader on May 27 and that on one occasion she pointed out Cordes to him. Blanc said that when Cordes learned that she was seeing Trader, he "seemed more nervous and moody than usual." But he never tried to talk her out of dating him.

Blanc also testified that in early May 1933, she ended the acquaintance with Cordes and urged him to return to his wife.

The District Attorney then presented evidence that Cordes had quarreled with his wife of several years for a divorce and even said he would marry Hazel if one was granted.

Hervey questioned the coworkers who saw Trader talking to the mystery man at the roller coaster. While all three admitted that Cordes bore a strong resemblance, none were positive it was him.

In total, the state called almost a dozen witnesses, each of whom were aggressively challenged by Hervey.

The defense called a handful of witnesses, but Gerhard Cordes exercised his right not to testify.

The jury received the case on Wednesday, September 20. They deliberated just twenty-seven minutes before declaring Cordes not guilty. As the verdict was read, a broad smile grew across Cordes's face. Mrs. Cordes, who was seated directly behind her husband, also smiled and appeared on the verge of tears.

Outside the courthouse, Gerhard Cordes told reporters: "No one knows better than I that I didn't commit the crime and I knew the jury would find me innocent. I think the speedy verdict exonerates me completely and I'll get back to work immediately on the police department if I can."

Chief John T. Peterson responded with a statement saying he wanted to review the case before asking the Civil Service Commission to lift the suspension. On September 20, 1933, Cordes formally requested the police department reinstate him. He argued that he had been acquitted in a court of law, was not guilty of murder and that the department had no legal right to deny his employment.

After Peterson consulted with City Manager Fred Lockwood, Cordes was given back his badge and gun on September 26. Assigned to patrol car duties on the 3:30–11:30 p.m. shift, he would be under the eye of Lieutenant George Sears at the La Jolla substation.

His employment didn't last long. On December 10, 1934, Cordes was fired for conduct unbecoming an officer after twenty-year-old Estelle Smith said Cordes burst into her apartment and beat her, then slashed her throat with a straight razor.

Smith told detectives she had begun her acquaintance with Cordes after he and his partner drove up on her at La Jolla Cove and Cordes struck up a conversation. Smith said she saw Cordes nearly every day afterward and that he had even spoken of love. She then told investigators how Cordes showed up drunk at her 846 Eleventh Avenue apartment and then savagely attacked her in a jealous rage.

After completing its investigation, the police department sent the case to the District Attorney and requested a warrant of arrest. Two days later, Cordes was booked into jail for assault with intent to commit murder. Shortly thereafter, he appeared without counsel and seemed unconcerned. Bail was set at $2,000 ($41,484 in today's dollars) pending a December 27 preliminary hearing.

According to the *San Diego Union*, while in jail, Cordes feigned being sick and injured and even wound up in the psychopathic ward, where he complained of suffering from prison psychosis. The court dismissed his ailments as stalling tactics.

On Thursday, January 10, 1935, Smith appeared with a heavily bandaged neck as she testified at Cordes's preliminary hearing to "a night of horror as a half crazed giant of a man" choked and then slashed her.

As Cordes sat in the courtroom with his wife, Smith testified that Cordes came stumbling into her apartment shortly after Officer Ed Stotler left. "He broke the glass on the door then reached in to turn the knob. After falling into the room and across my bed, he placed his arms around me and proceeded to call me endearing names. He wouldn't let go so I screamed. That's when Ed came in and I left the room."

According to reports, Stotler "knocked Cordes senseless" and then sent him home in a taxi. Cordes lived less than a mile away, at 530 Third Avenue.

Smith said, "About 11:30 he [Cordes] came back on my porch followed closely by his wife Lena." According to Smith, Lena said, "Do you know you have been the source of my unhappiness for more than a year now?"

Smith added that Gerhard placed his hands on her shoulders but that when she resisted, he knocked her down. She continued: "As Mrs. Cordes was applying a wet towel to my face, he came into the bathroom, threw me to the floor and slashed my throat with a razor. He was trembling and mumbling incoherent words. How I wrenched the razor from him and got out of the house I'll never know. I remember shouting at him with all my strength you're killing me but he paid no attention."

Smith then showed the court a vivid scar on the left side of her throat and a scar on one of her fingers.

During cross-examination, Attorney Edgar Hervy asked Smith, "Are you sure you and Mrs. Cordes didn't have a struggle over that razor that night?"

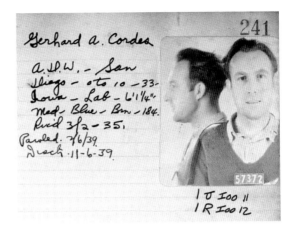

The San Quentin inmate card
of a disgraced former officer.
Courtesy San Quentin Archives.

"No of course not!" Smith insisted. "I think Mrs. Cordes is a fine woman." She added that Lena Cordes told her, "Gerhard would get what was coming to him for this." Smith then credited Lena with saving her life.

The preliminary procedure ended with Gerhard Cordes bound over for trial.

On February 12, 1935, with Edgar Hervey and his wife at his side, Gerhard Cordes stood before Judge Griffin and said he wished to admit his guilt and throw himself on the leniency of the court. Griffin accepted the plea and set February 21 for a probation hearing.

Cordes was ultimately sentenced to from one to ten years in San Quentin. He arrived at the massive stone-fortress-style penitentiary on March 2, 1935, where he remained until being paroled on November 6, 1939.

By that time, Lena Cordes had filed for divorce. Gerhard remarried soon after being released. The couple moved to the gulf coast of Texas in 1940, where he found work at the Houston Shipyard.

By the early 1950s, the San Diego region was experiencing a severe drought. By early 1952, Lake Hodges had run dry. On February 26, 1952, workmen under the north–south highway bridge connecting San Diego with Escondido came across a rusty handgun. When sheriff's deputies checked the serial number, they discovered it was the .38 revolver that had been reported stolen from Officer Alfred Schnepp in 1933.

The U.S. Constitution prohibits double jeopardy, so Cordes couldn't be rearrested for the Trader murder. But he was not without legal troubles. On July 23, 1952, Cordes was arrested by the Houston Police Department two hours after he stabbed Clara McCord to death with an icepick in her bathtub.

In confessing to the brutal slaying, Cordes blamed the thirty-eight-year-old divorcée for using him and kicking him out of her apartment. He asked detectives for "a quick execution."

On October 10, 1952, Cordes was convicted of murder and sentenced to the electric chair. The jury deliberated for less than forty minutes.

On March 18, 1953, the Texas Court of Appeals overturned the conviction on a procedural error. On November 20, 1953, Cordes was reconvicted and sentenced to life in prison. His sentence was affirmed by the same court of appeals on May 26, 1954.

Despite being sentenced to a life behind bars, Gerhard Cordes was paroled on November 28, 1968. He died a free man on May 1, 1987, in Austin, Texas.

8

THE COLDEST CASE

JULY 1933.

When seven-year-old Dalbert Aposhian and his best friend, ten-year-old Jackie Confar, decided to go out on a warm July day, no one thought twice of the pair heading Downtown. For the boys, the city center was their playground. They often caught a streetcar from their East San Diego homes and roamed through dime stores such as Woolworth's and Kress.

Dalbert lived at 4590 Forty-Seventh Street. His parents operated the Wardrobe Dry Cleaning and Tailor business at 1351 Fifth Avenue. Jackie's parents were furriers. Both stores were located on the north end of downtown, so the boys knew the area as well as their own neighborhoods.

Then, in the late afternoon of July 17, 1933, Dalbert went missing. At first, his parents drove the neighborhood looking for the youngster. They found nothing. A check of other friends' homes turned up negative results as well. By the time Sergeant Everett G. Fleming took the missing person report, George and Auda Aposhian were frantic.

Jackie told officers that the pair left their East San Diego homes and rode the streetcar west on University Avenue. After getting off at Park Boulevard and University Avenue, they walked south toward downtown. Jackie said he last saw Dalbert when they walked past the San Diego Zoo and his friend said he was going there.

Fearing another Virginia Brooks case, the police department response was massive. As missing person fliers were posted across the city, uniformed policemen checked every location between Fifth Avenue and the San Diego Zoo. Officers even visited every ice cream shop they could find.

According to the *San Diego Union*, the only possible clue was that the manager of the aircraft school on Fifth Avenue claimed to have seen Dalbert walk away at 5:00 p.m. when he told him to go home. No one else had seen him.

Then detectives thought they caught a break. Mrs. Pauline Guthrie of 4467 Forty-Fourth Street and Ruth Ahern of 4427 Central Avenue told Detective Sergeant Ed Dieckmann they saw the boy shortly after 8:00 p.m. on the day he went missing.

Guthrie said that Dalbert told them that he had relatives in La Jolla. Since "he aroused their sympathies," they gave him a ride to La Jolla.

Then came a conflicting story. W.J. Perkins of 3330 Thirty-Fourth Street claimed he saw Dalbert being forced into a car on Fairmount Avenue. Perkins said he saw the truck again later and noticed the driver shoving someone down onto the floor of the vehicle.

PL*ASE POST IN CONSPICUOUS PLACE

NOTICE   NOTICE   NOTICE   NOTICE

M I S S I N G   B O Y

DALBERT APOSHIAN

THIS BOY HAS BEEN MISSING SINCE 9 A.M. JULY 18, 1933. HE IS DESCRIBED AS FOLLOWS:

AGE 7 YEARS, DARK BROWN HAIR, BROWN (DARK) EYES, 45 LBS., HEIGHT 4 FEET, ONE INCH SCAR ON POINT OF CHIN. WEARING HOME-MADE BROWN-COLORED JACKET WITH PATCH OF SAME MATERIAL ON LEFT SIDE; LIGHT TAN SHIR WITH V-SHAPED COLLAR, KNOWN AS "BUSTER BROWN" TYPE; TAN-COLORED CORD TROUSERS, FADED FROM BEING WASHED; BROWN OXFORD SHOES, WITH STRAP AND BUCKLE ON TOP.

THIS BOY IS IN THE HABIT OF VISITING THEATER LOBBIES? TOY DEPARTMENTS OF STORES, ZOO, AND NATURAL HISTORY MUSEUM IN BALBOA PARK. LIKES TO BE IN PLACES WHERE PEOPLE CONGREGATE.

EVERY PERSON PLEASE PAY PARTICULAR ATTENTION TO THIS NOTICE AND MAKE EVERY EFFORT TO LOCATE THIS CHILD. IF HE SHOULD BE FOUND HOLD HIM AND CALL THE POLICE DEPARTMENT, FRANKLIN 1101.

HARRY J. RAYMOND,
CHIEF OF POLICE.

FK

Opposite: Downtown San Diego along Fifth Avenue in the late 1920s and early 1930s. Despite bustling with people and commerce, the area was generally safe for young, unaccompanied boys to explore. *Courtesy of San Diego Police Museum.*

Above: Missing person fliers were spread across the city as police hunted for Dalbert Aposhian. In the end, they generated nothing but false sightings. *Courtesy of San Diego Police Museum.*

That lead had the case agent, Detective Nathaniel J. McHorney—a veteran investigator and the last Chief of Police of the East San Diego Police Department before the municipality was absorbed by the City of San Diego a decade earlier—to consider the possibility that Dalbert had been kidnapped and was being held hostage.

The kidnapping theory was reinforced by a tip that said Dalbert had been seen in a rowboat headed to North Island. According to the tipster, the child was crying hysterically. A follow-up failed to locate the boat or anyone else who saw the child.

As expected, the search for the little boy evoked a wide range of emotions across the city. Some citizens complained. Others stepped up to help. Former SDPD Chauffer Frank W. Seifert offered three hundred volunteers from the American Legion to help the department in any way possible. If there was doubt as to his ability to get things done, a decade earlier, Seifert and three other men invented midair refueling while he was a member of the U.S. Army Air Corps.

The investigation officially shifted from a missing person case to a homicide case on July 23. Shortly after 7:30 a.m., four sailors assigned to Naval Station Coronado were on boat patrol in San Diego Bay when they spotted the badly mangled body of a child floating approximately one hundred feet off the Navy Pier. The sailors hoisted the boy into the boat and then motored to the pier to call the police.

The recovery confirmed everyone's worst fears. Nat McHorney was notified and sped to the scene. As soon as he saw the body, he summoned Chief of Detectives Harry Kelly. He in turn notified his boss, Chief of Police Harry Raymond. Within an hour, almost the entire police department was called back to work.

The press soon got wind of the grisly discovery. Within hours, "Extra, extra, read all about it! Maniacal killer slaughters his sixth victim!" was barked out on street corners across the city.

On July 24, Coroner Chester Gunn told the *San Diego Union*: "There is no doubt but that the little fellow was horribly murdered. There can be no mistake about the motive either. There is too much evidence for even a doubt."

When pressed by the media as to how the police department planned to solve the case, Chief Harry Raymond sarcastically responded, "We're going to do police work."

As expected, the find unleashed civic pandemonium. First, a local women's group demanded that "the city be cleaned out of its underworld gangsters, prostitutes, immoral dance halls, burlesque theatres, burglars and degenerates."

Detective Nat McHorney was the lead detective in the Aposhian case. The seasoned investigator passed away in 1956, never knowing the truth behind the death of the young boy. *Courtesy of San Diego Police Museum.*

Mrs. E.T. Hale, the president of California Congress Parent Teacher Association, told the *San Diego Evening Tribune*, "It would not be unreasonable to demand placing the county under martial law if the request of the women goes unheeded."

Harry Kelly responded: "My first hope is to find where he was slain. There's no doubt that it was done by a degenerate. We are tracing every known degenerate, men and women alike. We are doing everything that can be done. If this case is not solved it won't be the fault of this department."

The local media disagreed. First, the *San Diego Union* directly attacked the competency of the department's Homicide Bureau when it reported, "Six Murders, None Solved, Two Year Record."

Despite significant logistical differences in the cases, including the arrest and inexplicable acquittal of Garrett Moss, the *Union* implied that a serial killer was on the loose and that Dalbert Aposhian was his latest victim.

Then, on July 27, a *San Diego Evening Tribune* editorial stated that the police department was so controlled by City Hall politics that it was essentially paralyzed in solving the slayings. History would ultimately prove the political criticism warranted. Due to City Hall influence over what should be a political-free profession, eleven men served as Chief of Police from 1930 to 1940. The statistic is even more incredible when it's considered that George Sears served from 1934 to 1939.

Then came two more missing children. Mrs. Salvador Yepea reported her five-year-old daughter and four-year-old son missing from their home at 1879 Newtown Avenue. A team of officers conducted a ten-hour search of the neighborhood before finally locating the children safe and sound.

There had even been people turning in evidence of the killing. One woman who ran a downtown boardinghouse called police to report she'd found bloody linens in her rental and the tenant missing. It was later determined the linens were not related to the Aposhian case.

Detectives were becoming exhausted but remained determined as ever to crack the case. Then, two teenage boys came forward claiming that two men, E. Basset Curtis and Roy Thompson, showed them nude photos and "behaved inappropriately" as they were doing it. Curtis was soon arrested in Oakland. Thompson was personally arrested by George Sears and Ben Eichbaum in San Diego.

After aggressive questioning, both men were cleared as murder suspects but charged with their crimes against the young men.

On July 26, 1933, Marion Welcher, a twenty-one-year-old sailor stationed aboard the USS *Whitney*, was brutally stabbed just three blocks from Police Headquarters. The papers quickly proclaimed the attack the random work of a degenerate. In reality, Welcher was walking downtown when he accepted a ride from a man in a well-appointed Packard. At some point during the ride, the car's owner made a pass at Welcher and the two began fighting. Welcher survived his wounds, and the suspect was later arrested.

Then came the biggest news of all. On August 2, 1933, Los Angeles Police officers arrested nineteen-year-old Phillip Charles Edwards for loitering. The youth, just two weeks out of high school, quickly confessed to the police and even the *San Diego Union* to murdering Dalbert.

"Guess I was crazy when I did it," the young killer eagerly explained to newspaper reporters and Chief Kelly. He went so far as to say he took two years of law in high school and would defend himself in court.

The confession led Harry Kelly to inform the press thta the case was solved and the killer would be brought to justice.

But there was dissention within the police department. Chief Raymond, a veteran of more than twenty years of detective work when he was with the LAPD, had second thoughts. There were too many inconsistencies with Edward's confession, and the young suspect seemed too eager to tell the SDPD Bureau men what they wanted to hear.

Within days, Chief Raymond was telling the press he didn't think Edwards was the killer and that, despite the coroner's ruling, the death might not even have been a murder.

Dr. Frank Toomey, who conducted the autopsy, wasn't swayed. Declaring the murder weapon was probably a knife similar to those issued to sailors, he remained steadfast that Dalbert had been sodomized and mutilated before he was put in the water. Toomey

Chief Harry Raymond served in SDPD's top office for just ninety days, but his instincts that the Aposhian case was not a murder were ultimately proven right. *Courtesy of San Diego Police Museum.*

claimed to have found semen in the boy's rectum. There was no water in the boy's lungs, he noted during an inquest, and "all missing parts had been totally cut away and were not eaten by fish or crustaceans."

As the debate raged on regarding the cause of death to young Dalbert, the Detective Bureau, already stretched thin, found itself responding to an aggressive series of hot prowls, in which a night stalker type of bandit was breaking into homes across the city and robbing people at gunpoint. That series lasted fourteen months, until the bandit was killed by an Old Town shopkeeper's bullet.

Meanwhile, detectives from the San Diego County Sheriff's Department got involved with the Aposhian case. On two different occasions they interviewed Jackie; each time, his story remained the same. But Sheriff Ed Cooper publically stated that he had his doubts and surmised that Dalbert had fallen into the bay and drowned.

On September 19, 1934, Jackie was picked up downtown and taken to the Ocean Beach substation, where he was interviewed by District Attorney Investigator Thomas Frost and Monte Clark, a private detective hired by the Women's Committee of 600. The interview took place at the substation with Sergeant Jerry Lightner and District Attorney Thomas Whelan observing.

It was the fourth time Jackie had been questioned about his missing friend. According to the *San Diego Union*, as the interview was taking place, Jackie's parents, Mr. and Mrs. Arthur Confar, had no idea where he was and reported him as being kidnapped. Central Division officers were an hour into their search when they learned of the young boy's whereabouts.

After the re-interview with Jackie Confar, the youngster's story began to unravel. When pressed, Jackie admitted that he and Dalbert had gone to a pier to fish when they found a burlap sack and some melon rind to use as bait. As they were walking along the narrow wooden planks of the dock, Dalbert, who was holding the burlap sack, lost his balance and fell in. Fearing he would be in trouble, Jackie ran home and lied about what happened.

As soon as the sheriffs learned of the interview, they went to the man who conducted the autopsy, Dr. Toomey. He personally questioned Jackie about the incident, but his opinion didn't change. He still declared the case a murder.

Undaunted, Sheriff Ed Cooper hired a Los Angeles lab to demonstrate that sperm could not survive in water for six days. Dressing up rabbits in corduroy—what Dalbert was wearing when he died—forensic scientists inserted semen into their rectums and submerged them in crab cages.

Detectives delivered the results of the Los Angeles experiment to the police department, but the agencies still disagreed that the death was accidental, because of Dr. Toomey's autopsy.

On September 1, 1933, Chief Harry Raymond resigned to avoid being fired for ordering a bar owner arrested for selling liquor after midnight. Any direction for the police department to follow his theory that the Aposhian case was not a murder went with him.

Later that month, sheriff's detectives took the case to Toomey's boss, the Chief Medical Examiner of San Diego County, where they requested he personally evaluate the findings. After reviewing the Los Angeles experiment, the Medical Examiner agreed the injuries were caused postmortem by sea life and changed the death certificate.

The Police Department was unfazed. Perhaps because he was under enormous civic pressure to find what could be San Diego's first known serial killer, Harry Kelly stood by Dr. Toomey's autopsy and publically declared the case a murder. With two police agencies unable to agree, the case remained open but dormant for seventy-two years.

In 2005, Sheriff's Detective Curt Goldberg, relying on the expertise of Dr. Jon Lucas, a forensic pathologist at the San Diego Medical Examiner's Office, officially declared the cause of death as drowning and closed the case. "Since 1933, pathologists have learned a great deal more about what bodies look like after being submerged in water and attacked by marine life," Dr. Lucas told reporters. "The interpretation of homicide and abuse was based on a finding that's frequently seen on somebody that's been in the water for several days, where everything relaxes in the body, including the body's orifices. Sometimes they look like they've been violated but this was classic crustacean/fish activity." Dr. Lucas also noted that not all drowning victims have water in their lungs and sperm can't survive in open water for six days.

Van Aposhian was just eighteen months old when his brother died. He told the Associated Press that Dalbert's death greatly affected his family and that his parents died believing their son had been murdered. In a televised news conference, Van said his parents and his brother are together now, but it meant a lot to the remaining family to know the truth.

9

CELIA COTA

The sun was just setting over the picturesque Pacific coastline of San Diego when sixteen-year-old Celia Josephine Cota asked her younger sister Esther to accompany her on an evening stroll. It would have been the second outing for the sisters that evening. An hour earlier, at 7:00 p.m., they walked to a nearby post office to mail a letter.

The thirteen-year-old declined, saying she was tired and wanted to read a book. Despite Esther's refusal, Celia insisted on a walk.

The oldest daughter of a Mexican customs broker, Celia resided with her family in an older but well-appointed, two-story apartment building at 2779 "A" Street, a block south of Balboa Park in the hilly, tree-lined, tony neighborhood of Golden Hill.

Despite Celia seeming nervous and moody, the family had no way of suspecting it would be the last time they would see the four-foot, eight-inch, one-hundred-pound girl who had recently been voted the fairest of the fair at her high school.

Hours passed without Celia returning home. At first, her mother, Ophelia, figured she might have gone to her grandfather's home two blocks away. By midnight, panic began to set in, and Celia's father, Eduardo, called the police. Central Division patrolmen responded.

With a thick layer of ocean fog blanketing the quiet residential streets, prowl cars methodically combed the neighborhood for the young girl, clad in a white dress and yellow sweater.

Officers Ed Stotler and Leo Magone searched the house for clues as a patrol sergeant questioned the family for additional information.

Eduardo said Celia was under a doctor's care for extreme anxiety and would faint at the slightest scare. He said that the venture was the first time in her life that Celia had ever wanted to take a nightly stroll alone.

Esther was questioned on the chance that Celia had confided about meeting someone for a secret rendezvous. According to Esther, she had not.

Ophelia said that when Celia didn't return, she was gripped with a strange fear that her daughter was attacked near the home by a "sinister youth in a cap." Ophelia added, "I had a woman's intuition that she shouldn't be out alone but she smiled so brightly and seemed so cheerful that I just couldn't forbid her to go."

When asked if Celia had ever mentioned feeling threatened, Ophelia said two men who looked to be of "Japanese or Filipino descent" had followed her on several occasions.

After searching the house, Stotler and Magone turned to the backyard of the apartments. With the fog severely limiting their visibility, they found nothing.

As the morning sun rose and began to burn off the fog, the patrolmen started a second search. "Say. Wait a minute," Magone said as he grabbed his partner's arm and pointed toward a large chest. "Ain't that shoes or feet there? Behind that trunk?"

As the policemen gingerly approached the chest in the shrub-covered yard, their eyes began to focus on the horror of Celia's crumpled, ravaged

The backyard location where young Celia Cota was found behind a trio of tile-roof garages in the 2700 block of A Street, is relatively unchanged from the time of the brutal slaying.

body. She was lying on her back, and they could see that she had been severely beaten and that much of her blood-soaked clothing, including her underclothes, had been ripped from her petite body and discarded nearby. Clutched in her hands were clumps of gray hair.

As Stotler guarded the body, Magone, the senior officer, ran to the house to notify the Cota family and then telephone headquarters.

Lieutenant Joe Lopez, then serving as acting Chief of Detectives, was placed in charge of the investigation. A twenty-four-year veteran and often regarded as one of its premier investigators, Lopez immediately directed Detective Sergeant Fred "Jerry" Lightner and Detectives Ed Dieckmann and Frank Beaty to respond from home.

After learning of the murder, Sheriff Cooper called Chief of Police John T. Peterson and offered the assistance of Deputies William Gardner, Blake Mason, Boyd Moran and Earl Riley. Retired SDPD Detective Richard Chadwick Sr. heard about the killing on local radio and called Chief Peterson to offer his assistance. Within minutes, he was also on the case.

As detectives examined the crime scene, patrolmen set out on foot to locate possible witnesses.

According to the *San Diego Union*, Frank S. Fox, a city fireman stationed at the Twenty-Fifth and Broadway firehouse, reported seeing Celia walking north toward her family home between 8:15 and 8:30 p.m. According to the *Union*, Fox said he knew the Cota family personally and was positive it was her.

Officers also located Mrs. H.L. Dill of 1211 Twenty-Eighth Street, who said she thought her daughter heard a girl scream at 2:15 a.m.

Lieutenant Joe Lopez told the press that detectives surmised that Celia was returning home through the backyard when a chance prowler reached out from the dark and grabbed her. Blood splatter on the side of a rabbit coop confirmed the exact location of the attack. Unfortunately, it occurred in a part of the yard that was sheltered from view from the house by a garage.

The gray hairs in Celia's hand fueled a theory that the slaying could be connected to reports of an elderly man harassing girls in downtown movie theaters. Officers also followed up on reports of a man who had been spotted downtown several days earlier muttering "there are too many girls in San Diego. A few of them should be killed."

Shortly after Chief Peterson issued an order for officers to round up all known degenerates and convicted sex offenders, Joe Lopez told reporters, "I'm positive Miss Cota was struck by her assailant so quickly and without warning that she didn't have an opportunity to scream. She probably never knew what took place."

Left: Detective Lieutenant Joseph Lopez was widely regarded as the department's best investigator, but even he could not break the Cota case. *Courtesy of San Diego Police Museum.*

Right: Detective Sergeant Richard Chadwick came out of retirement to offer his investigative services to the Cota case. *Courtesy of San Diego Police Museum.*

Lopez added that it was highly unlikely the killer was associated with the family, as it was too risky to attack the girl so close to her home. Despite the public statement, Lieutenant Lopez had to consider every possible suspect. Within an hour of Celia being found, her seventeen-year-old boyfriend, Steve Rivera, was brought to headquarters for questioning. Lieutenant Lopez personally conducted the interview. Rivera said he and Celia regularly dated, but he was able to prove he was with Celia's aunt the night she went missing.

The autopsy was performed later that afternoon. As Dr. Frank Toomey and Dr. R.J. Pickard conducted the procedure, a videographer recorded their every move. It was the first time in San Diego history that a postmortem was filmed.

The autopsy concluded that Celia had been dead five or six hours when she was found. Bruising to the lower part of her face indicated the killer had large hands. The cause of death was strangulation, but the doctors detailed signs of suffocation, possibly with a coat. She had also been criminally assaulted. The gray hairs in her hand came from her pet rabbit.

News of San Diego's latest slaying spread like wildfire. Locally, radio stations KGB and KFSD broadcast the murder as part of the daily local news. Print media coverage of the crime stretched from coast to coast. With some newspapers calling Celia "Victim Number 7," the thought that a serial killer struck again sent a wave of panic across the city.

In addition to the pressure on police to solve the latest murder, the city planned to host the Balboa Park Exposition in 1935. The idea of a random serial killer hunting potential victims from thousands of tourists who flocked to the city was a nightmare scenario.

Another issue was vigilantes. More than one thousand angry men had heard the radio news of the killing and assembled outside the perimeter of the crime scene as detectives examined Celia's body. Packs of citizens looking for trouble may seem far-fetched by modern standards, but the Cota murder came less than a decade after a 1927 bank robbery in which half a dozen armed San Diegans opened fire on the bandits as they fled the scene.

Then things got worse. Shortly after midnight on August 20, thirty-five-year-old Mrs. E.L. Cross of 2530 J Street reported that a man attempted to attack her near where Celia was murdered. He fled after she screamed. She then ran to a nearby apartment, where she grabbed a milk bottle and hurled it at him.

Later that day, Lieutenant Lopez conceded: "We have no clues in the Cota case. The slayer left no track or trail. All we can do is hope for a break." Despite the deflated tone of his public statement, in private, Lopez and his detectives were working around the clock, reviewing evidence and interrogating potential suspects.

The August 21 *San Diego Union* reported the arrest of an unnamed Filipino at Third Avenue and Broadway after reports that the man had been "molesting women." The man was interviewed by Lieutenant Lopez, who determined he was not connected to the Cota murder.

One lead took investigators to the Mexican border, where they interviewed a known degenerate with a previous arrest for an attempted assault of a young girl in Balboa Park. Detectives learned the man had had a secret date with Celia just ten days before the murder, but he was able to prove he was in Mexico City on the night of the slaying.

After further questioning, Esther Cota admitted that her sister had confessed to a number of secret dates with men, including two sailors. But other than Steve Rivera, she couldn't provide their complete names.

Detectives tracked down the sailors but discovered that both were at sea when Celia was killed.

On Wednesday, August 22, nineteen-year-old laborer Paul Esparzo was arrested after the owner of the Rescue Mission witnessed him chase a fourteen-year-old girl into the restroom at the Rose Park playground at Eleventh and Island, then rub pepper in the girl's face and eyes. He was arrested several blocks away by Sergeant Harry Leetch and Detective Charles Padgett.

Esparzo was transported to Police Headquarters and was questioned by Sergeant Lightner about the Cota murder. It was determined that the pepper incident was a harmless prank and that he was not involved in the slaying.

Later that day, it looked like tragedy struck again. Nineteen-year-old Thelma Snodgrass, a schoolmate of Celia Cota's who resided less than two miles from the Cota home at 3335 Juniper Street, was reported missing by her family shortly after 11:00 a.m. According to Thelma's mother, the girl had no reason to vanish and had no money with her when she was last seen.

More than two dozen patrolmen swarmed the area, less than a mile east of Balboa Park, to search for the girl last seen dressed in a riding habit.

Thelma returned home the following day, saying she had hitchhiked to the central California town of El Centro and then spent the night in a motel before returning home around 6:00 p.m. The cause of her vanishing was related to a dispute over a dental appointment.

As officers cleared up the Snodgrass case, Detective Lieutenant George Sears was sworn in as SDPD's new Chief of Police following the retirement of John T. Peterson. It marked the second of three times Peterson would serve in the department's top office.

Immediately after receiving his gold chief's badge, Sears declared that solving the Cota murder was the department's top priority. He also stated that the police department would "be proactive in dealing with degenerates so to as to avoid future sex murders." The new Chief added, "Felony charges will be lodged against persons arrested for degenerate acts and upon conviction under a new state law they will be send to prison where they will be sterilized."

The inquest was held on Saturday, September 1. The hearing began as normal, but it had to be postponed for a day when several members of the Cota family became offended at the line of questioning.

Ophelia Cota was the first to testify. In regards to why Celia didn't immediately return home, she said her first thoughts were that she was either at a relative's home or was playing a prank. She added that she didn't know of anyone Celia would have left the house to meet.

When asked if a former convict who associated with Eduardo could be responsible for her murder, Ophelia stated, "I don't know anything about that."

Ophelia admitted she and Eduardo were estranged and he did not live in the home. It was not until his brother located him Downtown that he was even aware his daughter was missing. Eduardo returned to the family home around 10:30 p.m., but it wasn't until midnight when they finally called the police.

Among the most interesting testimony came from C.Y. Burcett, who resided in the apartment directly above the Cotas'. Burcett said he and his wife retired for bed at 11:30 p.m.

George Sears inherited the Cota case from outgoing Chief John T. Peterson. His case-management skills would be put to the test in another high-profile case two years later in La Jolla. *Courtesy of San Diego Police Museum.*

on the night Celia went missing. He said they did not see or hear anything unusual. "The first I knew anything was wrong was about 3 a.m. when I arose to go to work" Burcett testified. "At that time everyone was looking for the girl. I met Mr. Cota in the backyard and heard him tell another man something about 'I have an idea who did this.'"

Burcett said he helped in the search for a short time and then took his truck, which turned out to be parked just a few feet from where Celia's body was discovered, and went to work. He returned around 6:00 a.m., but Celia had still not been found. When asked about the large trunk in the backyard, Burcett insisted he had never seen it before. The trunk was treated for fingerprints, but no prints of value were located.

The inquest verdict read, "We find that Celia Cota came to her death at the hands of a person or persons unknown and we further find that she was brutally beaten and criminally attacked."

Celia's funeral was held on Tuesday, September 4, at Our Lady of Guadalupe Church at 1760 Kearny Avenue. With hundreds of mourners in

The teletype machine was a leap forward in information sharing between police agencies and played a part in disseminating information in the Cota investigation. The machines served the SDPD until being replaced by fax machines in the early 1980s. Today, the machine is a relic of the San Diego Police Museum. *Courtesy of San Diego Police Museum.*

attendance, it was one of the largest funerals in city history. Celia was laid to rest in Holy Cross Cemetery later that day.

On September 5, Las Vegas Police notified the SDPD that they had arrested thirty-one-year-old Lester E. Beard, alias C.E. Bower, in their jurisdiction after he attempted to attack a girl.

According to the *Los Angeles Times*, Beard had a criminal past, having served time in the Monroe Reformatory in Washington State for forgery. He had also been arrested in California, Nevada and Oregon. While serving time in an Oregon home "for the feeble minded," he had been sterilized.

The *Times* quoted Chief Sears as saying detectives had been looking for Beard since Celia's murder.

As rumors began to circulate among the inmates that Beard may have murdered an innocent girl, Clark County Sheriff Joe Keate and three heavily armed deputies stood guard inside the jail to protect him from the other inmates.

Meanwhile, Detective Sergeant Fred Lightner and Detective Frank Beatty headed to Las Vegas to interview him. During the interview, Beard denied ever being south of Los Angeles but later admitted he had been in San Diego when the murder took place. Beard also denied any involvement in the murder but, according to the *Times*, would scream and wring his hands whenever Celia's name was mentioned.

As promising as it all seemed, detectives were able to establish that Beard was not in San Diego when Celia was killed.

Shortly after completing an all-night interview, Detective Sergeant Lightner told the *Las Vegas Journal Review*: "Beard is definitely out as a suspect. We checked his alibi from every angle and find out that he was nowhere near San Diego on the night Celia was slain." Lightner went on to say, "We had an inkling of this before we left San Diego but we couldn't overlook a tip so we made the trip."

Ironically, one of the men able to prove Beard was not in San Diego was former Chief of Police Harry Raymond. Now working as a private investigator, Raymond, who once called Beard "the worst degenerate I have ever had dealings with," had tailed Beard north through California and then into Nevada when the murder occurred.

On September 15, Los Angeles Police arrested fifty-year-old Edward S. Schlacter, a self-employed gardener who lived just blocks from the Cota home. He had been missing since August 22 after reportedly boasting, "I know all about the Celia Cota murder" and "those dumb cops will never know what I know." Schlacter was transported to SDPD Headquarters, where he was interviewed by Lightner. Afterward, he was placed in the county psychopathic ward and eliminated as a suspect.

On October 8, 1934, Sergeant Lightner and Detective Ed Dieckmann questioned Mario Guidara, a thirty-two-year-old Filipino cook who had been arrested for an assault on a twelve-year-old girl in June 1934. Guidara was sleeping on the porch of a home at Twenty-Seventh and B Streets, approximately a block from the Cota home, when the murder occurred. He vanished three days later.

Dieckmann tracked down the homeowner, a single woman, who said she occasionally hired Guidara as a handyman, but she forbade him to sleep in the house.

Guidara insisted he fell asleep around 8:00 p.m. on the night Celia was killed. He explained that he left town three days later to find work in Los Angeles, where he was ultimately arrested and brought back to San Diego. Guidara denied having anything to do with the Cota slaying.

Without any evidence to refute his claims, the Guidara interview was labeled inconclusive.

On December 7, 1934, Detectives Charles Padgett and Olen Simmons booked twenty-eight-year-old Joe Herrera, a produce truck driver, for a brutal attack on five-year-old Patsy Jean Robertson. The child was asleep in her mother's bed in the family home at 149 Twenty-Ninth Street when Herrera broke in and attacked her.

Her mother, a nightclub hostess, found the little girl crying and bleeding when she came home around 11:00 p.m. on the sixth. The mother immediately called police, and the little girl was transported by the police ambulance to County Hospital.

Detectives learned Herrera was a frequent visitor to the Robertson home and knew Patsy by sight. She also knew him. As Patsy lay in her hospital bed, detectives brought Herrera into the hospital room for her to identify. Sitting up in her bed, the little girl cried out, "That's him! That's the man who hurt me," when she saw Herrera.

Despite the identification, Herrera maintained his innocence, claiming he was asleep in his home at 2856 Imperial Avenue when the assault occurred.

Detectives Padget and Simmons visited the home, where Herrera lived with his mother. She contradicted her son and said he was not home on the night Patsy was assaulted. The mother added that she was out looking for Joe about the same time the attack occurred.

On December 9, Sergeant Lightner told the press that in addition to the charges of attacking the little girl, the department was also looking into whether Herrera was a suspect in the Cota case. "We haven't finished questioning Herrera by any means," said Lightner, adding that he would probably be seeking a criminal complaint on Monday morning.

Despite extensive questioning by both Lightner and Harry Kelly, Herrera adamantly denied being involved in either crime. Charges of assaulting Patsy were officially filed on December 11, and a preliminary hearing was set for December 24. Trial was set for the following month.

Then came a bombshell. On January 24, 1935, Herrera walked out of court a free man when Judge Lloyd Griffin ruled there was insufficient evidence to hold him. Griffin had spent more than an hour trying to calm the sobbing girl, without success. He finally turned to the four-man, eight-woman jury and said, "There is sufficient medical evidence to show the girl has been attacked but as long as she is unable to take the witness stand the jury cannot receive sufficient evidence to convict."

By February 1935, the police department had questioned more than 150 men, including some hundreds of miles away, who could have been involved in the Cota slaying. In every case, the results were either solid alibis or inconclusive.

In April 1935, thirty-year-old Thomas Dugger, a San Antonio native who once served time in Texas for stabbing a police chief, was arrested for a series of "ape man" attacks in Los Angeles. In each case, Dugger attacked women from behind and viciously strangled them.

After learning of the arrest, Chief of Detectives Harry Kelly sent a teletype to LAPD Captain Bert Wallis, requesting additional information on Dugger, specifically, if he was in San Diego around the time Celia was murdered.

During the subsequent interrogation, LAPD Detectives noted that despite being small in stature and soft spoken, Dugger "gesticulated wildly with his gnarled and sinewy hands" as he gleefully confessed how, on three occasions, he had been overcome with an "irresistible impulse" to savage women. Despite his enthusiastic confessions, Dugger denied any involvement in the Cota slaying.

If Dugger lied about being the one who killed Celia, he took the secret to his grave. He was hanged on May 1, 1936, after being convicted under the "Little Lindbergh" kidnapping law. The execution marked the first time in California history that a person was put to death for a crime other than murder.

On February 29, 1936, the Sheriff's Department told the *San Diego Union* that it was seeking information on thirty-one-year-old James Pearl from their counterparts in San Bernardino. According to Deputy Herb Kennedy, Pearl, who routinely traveled with craft shows, had been arrested for a criminal attack on a thirteen-year-old girl in their jurisdiction. Kennedy said they were most interested in his whereabouts at the time Celia was murdered. Like all of the other seemingly interesting leads in the case, this, too, was a dead end.

On June 27, 1937, the *San Francisco Chronical* highlighted the still-unsolved murder and said Celia was "the 6th victim of a modern day Jack the Ripper."

The Celia Cota murder case is still open and unsolved.

One bit of spooky irony is that, prior to the Cota family moving to 2794 A Street, they resided at 950 Fourteenth Street. The house is long gone, but the location is now the west side of San Diego Police Department Headquarters. Two stories below where the home once stood is Celia's case file, housed inside a storage vault of old murder cases.

10

A GUILTY CONSCIENCE

AUGUST 31, 1936.

I t was shortly after 9:30 a.m. when Mrs. Edith Gurtler of 8654 Coast Boulevard was walking Foust, her wirehaired fox terrier, along the picturesque La Jolla coastline when she discovered the brutalized body of a middle-aged brunette at the foot of Cuvier Street.

She raced to a phone and called the police. Her call was received at 9:10 a.m., and a prowl car was dispatched from the La Jolla substation at 1035 Prospect Street, approximately a half mile away.

Officer Edward Herting Jr. was first on scene. "Foust started barking and tugging at his leash" Mrs. Gurtler told the policeman. "I unleashed him and he raced down into a gully out of sight. I thought he was being bothered by bees so I followed."

Gurtler continued: "The first thing I saw was a woman under a palm tree. I couldn't imagine why she should be lying with the sun in her face and on the lower right side of her body. Approaching I saw the woman was dead, in rigor mortis, for one hand was above her bosom without touching her body. The right knee was bent stiffly, and the left leg stuck out on the ground."

Herting's report noted that the woman's dress had been pulled up and her underclothing removed. The body had been severely beaten, most likely with a bloody wooden club that had been discarded ten feet to the right of her body. Clutched tightly in her fists were clumps of black hair, possibly indicating that she fought her assailant. Dried blood under her fingernails suggested she put up a valiant fight.

A late 1930s photo of the sleepy main road into La Jolla suggests how small and isolated the picturesque seaside neighborhood was at the time of the Muir slaying. *Courtesy of San Diego Police Museum.*

Officer Herting radioed to the La Jolla sub to notify the Chief and to send homicide detectives to the scene. Moments after being notified, Chief George Sears ordered Detective Ed Dieckmann to drive to La Jolla and assume command of the investigations.

Dieckmann's case notes record that he made the sixteen-mile drive from Police Headquarters and met Officer Herting and Deputy Coroner A.E. Gallager less than thirty minutes later.

Sears's experience with the 1931 summer of murders told him that the latest killing would quickly erode into a media circus—especially given that it occurred in the upscale, somewhat isolated community of La Jolla, where violent crime was virtually unheard of.

If the police department wanted to maintain control of the investigation and keep the public reassured that the city was still safe, Sears needed a massive, highly visible response.

Internally, Sears would have to answer if the latest murder was related to the fiendish unsolved slayings of Virginia Brooks, Louise Teuber, Dalbert Alphonsian and Celia Cota.

Sears ordered all officers on days off or on vacation to report for duty. He then ordered Chief of Detectives Harry Kelly to transfer eight men from the vice squad, who routinely interacted with San Diego's seedy underworld, to the murder case. Kelly was then instructed to relocate his office from downtown to the La Jolla substation.

Lieutenant Jack Berg was placed in change of the remaining plainclothesmen in the downtown bureau.

By the end of the day, more than sixty officers had been detailed, including three assigned exclusively to staff an established tip line at the La Jolla substation.

Official police reports indicate that there were several items of interest at the crime scene, including a pool of blood located near a white wooden Japanese-style gateway twenty yards from where the body was located.

A young boy had located a cork-and-fiber sun helmet floating in the ocean approximately 250 feet from the murder scene. According to Ed Dieckmann's notes, Ruth's family would later identify the helmet as belonging to the murdered woman.

Detective Sergeant Ralph Whitney filed a report that stated a married couple who lived just two hundred feet from where the body was found

The small La Jolla substation at 1033 Wall Street was the center of activity for the Muir murder investigation. In 1937, it was replaced by a larger substation at 7877 Herschel Street. *Courtesy of San Diego Police Museum.*

heard two "moaning cries" around 10:00 p.m. The woman said that as she listened, a small gray car "came along Coast Drive" and stopped opposite the wall that hid the murder scene. The machine remained for only a moment then drove away heading south.

Several officers filed reports of a "burly male who smelled of intoxicating liquor" walking near the old Scripps Garden around 9:45 p.m. Beyond a basic clothing description, no one could provide information that could identify him.

As patrolmen checked the community for witnesses, they also noted angry mobs forming. The groups were disbursed, only to reassemble at another location. The victim was identified by a missing person report as forty-eight-year-old Ruth Sackett Muir, an unmarried secretary for the Riverside YWCA.

According to Dieckmann's cases notes, the missing person call came into the La Jolla substation at 12:15 a.m. and patrolmen began an immediate search of the area. Downtown was also notified. Officers spent the rest of the night searching. Despite a full moon illuminating the streets, they found nothing.

Detectives learned that Ruth had vacationed in La Jolla every year since 1930 and was staying in a rental cottage at 324 Prospect Street, roughly three blocks from where she was killed. According to her elderly parents, who had accompanied her, Ruth was last seen at 9:30 p.m. when she invited them to join her for a walk along the ocean.

According to his case notes, Dieckmann interviewed eighty-four-year-old Joseph Muir, a wealthy retired banker, shortly after Ruth was identified. When questioned about the last time he saw his daughter, Joseph told Dieckmann: "I told her I was too tired to join her on the walk. At first I tried to convince myself no harm could come to her in this area but when she did not come home an hour later we became uneasy and a little later we notified police."

A subsequent report filed by Dieckmann clarified why the search did not find Ruth earlier. "As soon as I saw the body I knew why it had not been discovered earlier. Along the cliffs, at the foot of Cuvier Street and opposite Scripps Gardens the scenic drive is bordered by a stone retaining wall that follows the curve of the shore line. Between the wall and cliff edge there runs a dirt path, and beyond this the rocky surface has been covered with soil, planted with shrubs and terraced to form nooks where observation benches are located. At one time there had been a sunken goldfish pond at the bottom of a twenty five foot depression. The sides of the depression were covered with a thick growth of clinging ice plant. Set into the cement cornice of the pool were five white painted lengths of pipe, once used as standards for a fence. In the center of the spot enclosed by the pipes and hidden from all sides but one, lay the body of the slain woman."

By midnight on September 1, all of California and Baja Mexico was on alert for a killer. Hours later, the Tijuana Police Department reported that Isaac Levy, an English merchant marine, had encountered a man who confessed to murdering Ruth. Dieckmann and Whitney were sent to Tijuana Police Headquarters to interview Levy. The *San Diego Union* reported that the entire thing was a hoax after Levy admitted to police, "I hoped if I did something valuable I would be invited to stay in the United States as a citizen."

The September 2, 1936 *San Diego Union* declared, "Police and Sheriff's officers, who have hunted in vain for perpetrators of similar crimes in the San Diego region in recent years, threw their entire resources into the search for the killer believing they are hunting a fiend with a lust for killing."

Harry Kelly's response was vague. "We believe someone away from La Jolla, possibly of San Diego, committed the crime."

As media coverage grew, Chief Sears ordered more policemen on the case. Specialized fingerprint examination equipment was delivered to the La Jolla substation, and additional phone lines were installed to handle tips.

Dr. Toomey conducted the postmortem on September 3. His examination determined the cause of death as multiple skull fractures and manual strangulation. The hair and blood found under Ruth's fingernails came from her own head, most likely as she flailed her arms to protect herself. The blood on the club, which measured fourteen inches long by one and one-eighth inches thick and two and five-eighths inches wide, also belonged to Ruth. Despite her underclothing being removed, Ruth had not been criminally attacked.

On September 7, 1936, Henry W. Coil, the president of the Riverside Kiwanis Club, sent a telegram to Governor Frank Meriam requesting he use his power as the chief executive of California to request the assistance of the FBI in handling the case. "Seventh unsolved sex murder occurred last Monday when Miss Ruth Muir talented and popular secretary of Riverside YWCA was ravished and slain at La Jolla. Local police report no substantial progress made toward discovery of the perpetrator. Proximity Mexican border indicates the probability of chronic interstate crime condition which together with large naval establishment at San Diego amply justifies interposition Federal Bureau of Investigation and indignant Riverside citizens request you immediately call G-Men into the case."

New Link in San Diego Death Chain

How long will shadowy death strike at women and girls in and around San Diego? That is what police are wondering as they seek to solve the latest of the mysterious slayings—that of Ruth Muir, Riverside Y.W.C.A. secretary, near La Jolla, the seventh in the San Diego area in as many years. In each case investigation has led to a blank wall. The dread toll of unsolved murder mysteries in and around San Diego includes the murder of Lois Kentle of Los Angeles and her fiance, Francis Conlon, stabbed to death on the Ensenada, Mexico, beach, Aug. 26, 1930; Virginia Brooks, 10, abducted and slain at San Diego, Feb. 14, 1931; Louise Teuber, hanged near San Diego, April 18, 1931; Mrs. W. B. (Dolly) Bibbens, strangled in her San Diego apartment, April 23, 1931; Hazel Bradshaw, stabbed in Balboa park, San Diego, May 2, 1931, and Celia Cota, 16, choked to death in San Diego, Aug. 18, 1934. (Central Press photos)

Despite differing wildly from other cases, shortly after the news broke of the Muir slaying, the press pushed forward a theory that Ruth Muir's murder was the work of a single fiendish killer.

A.A. Piddington, the editor of the *Press Enterprise*, also telegraphed the governor urging the assistance of the FBI. He then personally called Congressman Sam Collins, demanding federal assistance.

Meanwhile, Chief Sears reported that SDPD had accepted the assistance of San Diego County sheriff's deputies with what was becoming the crime of the year.

Sears told the press that more than thirty suspects had been brought in for questioning, including several who wanted to confess to the crime. But all had been released due to a lack of corroborative evidence.

One of the men questioned was twenty-six-year-old Wilbert Felix Friend. A transient who worked as a golf caddy at the La Jolla Country Club, Friend lived in a tent at the foot of Pearl Street, less than a mile from the crime scene.

Officers discovered his tent when it was unoccupied. After impounding two suitcases, a gasoline stove and a camp cot, they left a note inside for the owner to come to the La Jolla substation if he wanted his items back.

On September 14, Friend claimed his items, saying he had been in the Laguna Mountains for the past two weeks. His wife backed up the alibi. Friend was questioned but admitted nothing that connected him to the crime. After it was determined that the items impounded from the tent had no evidentiary value, he was released but chalked up as a sexual deviant.

On September 21, Officer Ed Stotler and Deputy Walter Blue traveled to Patton State Hospital for the Criminally Insane, located in an unincorporated community in San Bernardino County, to interview thirty-year-old inmate Don Hazell. Hazell was originally arrested on September 4 after being spotted outside the inquest hearing being held at the La Jolla Memorial Chapel. Muttering incoherently about the Muir murder, Hazell alarmed passersby, who called the police.

Described as "a gorilla of a man" standing six feet, one inch and weighing 245 pounds, Hazell was transported to the La Jolla substation, where he was questioned by Detective Sergeant Jerry Lightner.

At one point, Lightner asked Hazell, "How old are you?"

"I'm 8 years old," Hazell replied.

"Aren't you kind of big for your age?" Lightner quipped.

According to Lightner's report, Hazell's responses ranged from ambling and incoherent to strange and bewildering.

In the Patton Hospital interview, Hazell told Stotler and Blue that he purchased liquor in La Jolla on the afternoon of August 31, then spent the rest of the day drinking. That night, he saw Ruth alone, standing behind a bench. Armed with a bottle, Hazell said he struck Ruth in the head, knocking her to the ground. Afterward, Hazell said he stood over Ruth and cut off her corset with a pocketknife but was then scared away.

"What did you do with the bottle?" Stotler asked.

"I threw it in the ocean when I ran away."

On the surface, the confession appeared legitimate. Absent the inconsistency of the murder weapon, Ruth was alone and near a bench when she was attacked. The injuries to her head suggested she had been struck from behind. A microscopic examination of the corset revealed it had been cut with a sharp instrument.

After the murder, Hazell said he hitchhiked to his parents' home at 2722 Union Street, just north of downtown San Diego.

His family had a different story. Mr. and Mrs. Hazell told Stotler that except for a morning visit to a barber and an afternoon trip to the cleaner's, their son was home all day on the thirty-first. Frances Hazell added that she had seen Donald as late as 9:00 p.m., when she went to bed.

Squads of officers fanned out across La Jolla to show Hazell's picture to bus drivers, motorists, store owners and anyone else who could have seen him in La Jolla on the thirty-first. According to Ed Dieckmann's notes, they found no one.

When contacted for a statement, Patton Superintendent Eugene M. Webster bluntly told the *San Diego Evening Tribune*: "Hazell is insane. He will confess to anything."

Ninety miles north of downtown San Diego, Riverside County Sheriff C.F. Rayburn and Undersheriff Steve Lynch were investigating the case from their jurisdiction. Forty-two-year-old Fred Wurthen, a transient from Visalia, had been arrested after reportedly boasting of "seeing Miss Ruth Muir murdered by his partner."

When he was searched by Riverside deputies, Wurthen had in his possession a San Diego map as well as a woman's breastpin, a compact, a billfold and a set of keys.

After an inconclusive interview with Wurthen, in which the inmate steadfastly denied being in San Diego or knowing anything about the slaying, Sheriff Rayburn had the prisoner photographed and fingerprinted. He was also examined for bruises and scratches, and a hair sample was collected. The evidence was then sent to Harry Kelly in San Diego.

The Muir murder remained unsolved for almost nineteen years when, shortly after 10:30 p.m. on May 28, 1955, a husky-voiced man called the *San Diego Union* night desk and told reporter Mark Waters that he wanted to confess to killing a woman named Muir back in 1936.

The crime was so old that the thirty-five-year-old Waters, a native of Baltimore, knew nothing about it. Unsure if he was speaking to a legitimate criminal or a crackpot living out a homicidal fantasy, Waters telephoned the *Union*'s crime beat reporter at SDPD Headquarters to ask if he knew anything about the crime.

Waters ran to the *Union*'s library, where he located dozens of clippings about the 1936 slaying in a file dubbed "The Unsolved Enchantment Murder at La Jolla by the Sea."

Waters then called the SDPD Homicide Bureau. As he was on the line, the confessor called back.

"It's Friend again."

In a follow-up interview with the *San Diego Union*, Waters described the phone call in detail. He recounted that he recognized the voice as the same person who had called earlier. "I want to see you tonight. Not tomorrow. Come up here yourself and get me."

"Alright," Waters replied. "You stand up there and I'll come up and get you. It'll take me an hour or so."

"Did you tell the police?"

"No."

"You're a liar!" the caller responded angrily. "You've got every cop in the state looking for me right now."

Knowing that Detective Sergeant Paul Walk was on the other line attempting to trace the call, Waters had to stall.

"How can I tell it's you?"

"I'm wearing a white shirt and gray pants. I have a mustache. I'll be waiting for you."

Waters later told detectives, "I don't know what made me believe him. Usually on a Saturday night a newspaper switchboard gets at least a dozen crank calls."

The phone company traced Wilbert Felix Friend's call to a phone booth inside a San Juan Capistrano hotel. Walk quickly relayed the address to the Orange County Sheriff, who dispatched two deputies. They arrived just in time to grab Friend as he walked out of the booth. Friend offered no resistance. He was held at a sheriff's substation until Walk could make the seventy-mile drive to get him.

With seventeen years on the force, Sergeant Walk had enough investigative experience to know people will sometimes make false confessions. After introducing himself, Walk asked Friend, "Why do you want to confess now?"

"I'm tired of running. I need to get this off my chest and clear my conscience. I have nothing to live for anymore. I want to die."

If you want to die," Walk countered, "why didn't you just commit suicide?"

According to Walk's case notes, Friend seemed put off by the question. "Because committing suicide is wrong," he finally replied.

The slightly built Friend then confessed that he had been drinking heavily on the night of the killing. Having lost all his money playing pool, Friend said he was looking for someone to rob when he came upon Ruth sitting alone on a bench overlooking the Pacific Ocean. After wrenching a leg from a nearby picnic bench, Friend said he crept up and struck her in the head. After killing Ruth, he searched her purse but found it was empty. He then left the body in a gully. Friend added that he stayed in La Jolla for five days after the slaying.

Walk drove Friend back to San Diego and booked him in the County Jail at 4:00 a.m.

A team of investigators led by Detective Lieutenant Mort Geer learned that Friend was no stranger to the justice system. In 1937, he served ten months on a road camp work crew after a burglary conviction. In 1939, he was sentenced to eighteen months behind bars for lewd and lascivious conduct with a child. The sentence also required Friend to register as a sex offender.

In 1942, Friend was arrested for rape. Under the terms of his twenty-five-year probation, he was ordered to undergo an orchidectomy, a medical procedure in which his testicles were removed.

Geer told reporters that Friend had confessed twice to the killing and had even told his sister-in-law about the crime a few days before he called the newspaper. The sister-in-law said at the time that she didn't believe him.

Geer added that Friend was in San Juan Capistrano placing flowers on his mom's grave when he finally decided to break down and confess. Geer said Friend even went so far as to accompany Sergeant Walk and Detective Robert Creason to La Jolla, where he reenacted the night of the slaying.

What Geer didn't tell the press was that his detectives also questioned Friend extensively about the other unsolved killings but found nothing linking him.

Days later, Mark Waters met with Friend at the County Jail. He later wrote, "At that time I had my exclusive. I had a lot of facts no other reporter would have. I was all set to write it. But there was a question that wasn't answered. Why did it take Friend 19 years to confess?"

With Wilbert Friend in custody, Lieutenant Mort Geer (*left*) and Chief of Detectives Graham Roland examine the makeshift club he used to savagely kill Ruth Muir almost twenty years earlier. *Courtesy of San Diego Police Museum.*

Waters continued: "I met Friend in his cell. He was on his cot, slumped forward a bit. He chain smoked throughout our entire talk. He greeted me with a smile and said, 'Oh, you must be the guy.'

"I asked him my question and this is how he answered me, 'I had a wife. She was a good woman and I loved her. We were happy together. She was fine and she made me forget things, bad things of the past. She died a couple of years ago and from that time on I felt like confessing. Three or four times I almost went to a newspaper or the cops but each time I lost my nerve. Then, a few weeks ago, my mother died. I was at her grave and I prayed to God. I thought of how I wanted to walk into the gas chamber and die. That's when I called you mister.'"

On June 2, 1955, Lieutenant Geer stamped "CANCELED" on the front of the twenty-three-inch-thick Ruth Muir murder file. It had been eighteen years, eight months and one day since the brutal killing.

The same day, just after 2:00 p.m., Friend stood before Judge Ronald Abernathy and told him he did not need a lawyer. Friend said, "I killed her. I plead guilty, let it go away."

"I will not accept your plea," the judge responded. "This is a case punishable by death. You must have an attorney to advise you." The judge then appointed former Deputy District Attorney John R. Sorbo to represent Friend. As Judge Abernathy stated his decision, Detective Lieutenant Ed Dieckmann, now retired, was sitting in the front row of the courtroom listening intently.

In his opening statements at Friend's murder trial, Sorbo conceded that his client killed Muir. But he told the five-man, seven-woman jury that since there was no premeditation, no robbery and no sexual assault, they should convict Friend of second-degree murder.

On August 4, 1955, the jury delivered a guilty verdict of first-degree murder without recommendation for mercy. Knowing the verdict meant death in the San Quentin gas chamber, Friend leaped from his seat and bolted toward the door. After being tackled by Deputies Michael Irving and Richard Buchanan, Friend was escorted into a tunnel and led back into the County Jail.

Friend later told reporters that he thought by confessing the jury would have been more lenient. He added, "If I had to do it all over again, I wouldn't have confessed. It caused too much fuss for my friends and relatives."

As with every condemnation case, the sentence was automatically appealed to the California Supreme Court. The court affirmed the first-degree murder conviction but sent the case back for a retrial on the penalty. The second jury ordered death. The penalty was again appealed to the California Supreme Court, which affirmed the death recommendation on a four-to-three vote.

On September 13, 1958, Friend met with reporters at San Quentin and said he was prepared to die. "I want to get this over with," the condemned man stated. Friend added that the date with the gas chamber would be a lot better than a life sentence behind bars. His only complaint was a fear that the October 10 execution would somehow be delayed.

"It's happened to other guys," Friend said. "Just sitting around all day thinking about it can drive you crazy. I'm anxious to go. I've been sitting here for three years waiting for it to be over and most of the time not knowing when it will be. I'm waiting for October 10th. It's all I can think about."

Friend then wondered aloud as to whether heaven or hell existed and complained that he received only one birthday card when he turned forty-eight on August 30. "I opened the card, it was from someone in San Diego and it read 'another 365 days shot to hell'."

He concluded the interview by saying that, had he known how much damage he would have done to other people's lives, he would not have killed Muir.

On October 8, 1958, Governor Goodwin Knight, acting on a petition filed by Sorbo, commuted the death sentence to life without parole. It was forty-eight hours before Friend was scheduled to die. Friend told reporters he was happy with the governor's action.

11

A HOMICIDAL IRONY

DECEMBER 21, 1945.

Thirty-six-year-old John Harvey Latham was an average family man who ran a Barrio Logan salvage yard and tire shop at 2190 Main Street. He was married with four young children: John (age six), Patrick (four), Jacqueline (two and a half) and Robert (three months). The family resided at 4584 West Point Loma Boulevard. in the Loma Portal District.

John was born in Los Angeles but had resided in San Diego since 1925. A Point Loma High School graduate, he operated a filling station on Rosecrans Street and Canon prior to purchasing the salvage yard.

The last contact anyone had with John was when he phoned his wife, Helen, at 8:57 p.m., saying he had just made a late sale and would then be leaving the shop.

John routinely carried between $400 and $500 ($6,100 and $7,200 when adjusted for inflation) in cash in addition to the several hundred dollars in the day receipts he would bring home in a canvas bag.

When he didn't come home by morning, Helen dismissed it as a habit of "staying out with the boys." What she didn't know was that his body had been found by Frank O. Flinn of 2004 C Street, an employee opening up the business.

Uniformed patrol officers responded soon after Flinn's emergency call was received in the Police Department's business office at Police Headquarters, now located at 801 West Market Street.

All that remains of the Latham murder scene is a slight rise in the cement that was once the floor of his office. Today, the location is occupied by Fire Etc., a first-responder supply company.

As the patrolmen examined the body, lying in a pool of blood underneath an open front shed just off the main office, they discovered extensive head trauma. The patrolmen phoned headquarters with their findings to ask that detectives respond.

Detective Lieutenant Ed Dieckmann assigned Detectives Elmer Wadman and Charles D. Hughen to investigate. Both men had extensive experience with death investigation.

Flinn told Detectives Wadman and Hughen that he last saw John when he left the shop at about 5:30 p.m. on December 20. Flinn said that when he arrived at work at his usual time, shortly after 7:00 a.m., he noticed a light still burning in the front office. That was unusual. So was the fact that the front gate to the business had been left open.

Flinn said that as he went to turn on the electric tire mold, he saw John's car in the yard. Seconds later, he found his boss dead. A clock connected to the tire mold machine had stopped at 8:50 p.m., indicating that John had turned off the appliance shortly before calling his wife.

The detectives concluded that John had changed from his work attire into his street clothes and was struck on the back of his head as he stepped out of the office into the equipment-loaded shed.

The body fell face downward, but the killer apparently rolled John onto his back. The primitive gravel floor of the shed showed no signs of a struggle. A search of the business revealed no cash on hand; the customary large amount that John carried was also missing.

Later that morning, Lieutenant Dieckmann met with reporters. He said that John was killed by a single strike to the head that crushed his skull.

The lieutenant added that the blow was rendered by a thirty-three-inch section of two-inch rusty pipe that had been left at the scene. Dieckmann said there were no other clues and opined that the pipe was probably too rusty to retain fingerprints—a fact later reinforced by a lab examination of the weapon.

Dieckmann also revealed that detectives believed robbery was the motive of the murder. Dieckmann theorized that someone saw John counting out the day's receipts and that the attack was not preplanned.

Later that morning, Detectives Wadman and Hughen arrested twenty-five-year-old Robert Sewell of 2184 Logan Avenue. A former employee hired to recap and change tires at the shop, Sewell had been fired by John Latham just a few days

In his later years, Elmer Wadman was one of San Diego's preeminent forensic consultants and often testified as an expert in crime scene investigations. *Courtesy of San Diego Police Museum.*

earlier. After transporting Sewell to Police Headquarters, Wadman and Hughen questioned him about his activities on the evening of December 20.

Sewell said he left the hotel about 7:00 p.m. and went to lower Fifth Avenue, where he visited several cafés, "had drinks with several colored men," then returned two hours later. Sewell said that soon thereafter he again left the hotel to get food for his wife and came back about 11:30 p.m. and went to bed. Sewell insisted he knew nothing about the slaying.

As detectives interrogated Sewell at headquarters, Latham was taken to Johnson Saum Mortuary, where an autopsy was conducted under the direction of Deputy Coroner A.E. Turner. The postmortem concluded that Latham died of "a crushing skull fracture, apparently the result of a very vicious blow from a blunt instrument."

With no corroborative evidence linking him to the slaying, the investigators had no choice but to release Sewell and move on with the investigation.

John Latham was laid to rest in Holy Cross Cemetery.

Despite letting Sewell leave headquarters after questioning, Wadman and Hughen still needed to verify his alibi. Detective Sergeant William "Bert"

Lieutenant Walter Scott, head of the SDPD crime lab. Despite its best efforts, Scott's team could not recover any valuable evidence off the murder weapon. *Courtesy of San Diego Police Museum.*

Ritchey and Detective Jack Bransford, both African American officers, visited several saloons on lower Fifth Avenue that catered to a mostly Black clientele. No one remembered seeing Sewell.

On January 23, 1946, an inquest revealed that John Latham died of a depressed skull fracture caused by the result of three strikes to the head. Among those who testified was the head of the SDPD crime lab, Lieutenant Walter Scott, who confirmed that the murder weapon was so degraded that it was impossible to obtain identifiable fingerprints from it.

Despite the best efforts of detectives and the crime lab, there was simply not enough evidence to pursue the case, and it fell dormant.

After three years, it began to appear as though the case would be forever unsolved. Then came a break. On January 18, 1949, Sewell returned to San Diego, where he was arrested on a charge of drunkenness and suspicion of robbery.

Two days later, on the morning of January 20, Sewell was escorted into the Police Court, where he pled guilty to the charge of drunkenness. Judge John Brennan sentenced him to twenty days in custody with one day suspended.

It was then learned that the drunkenness arrest was a ruse. On January 2, 1949, Stockton, California police had contacted the SDPD Homicide Bureau with very detailed information about the three-year-old murder from Robert Massey, a close friend of Robert Sewell's. The police department brought Massey to San Diego for questioning, and on January 20, Detective Sergeant Russell Ormsby interviewed him about the crime.

Seven hours later, Ormsby learned that Sewell had confessed to Massey that he went to the tire shop on the night of December 20 with the intent to burglarize the place. Massey said Sewell told him that he "had hit" the decedent.

Using Massey's information, Detective Sergeants Anthony Maguire and Ormsby went into the city jail and again questioned Sewell about the night of December 20, 1945. Sewell again denied any involvement. He insisted he had visited several restaurants and pool halls that evening and had engaged in a dice game in which he won eighty-seven dollars. Sewell again claimed he returned to his hotel room at about 11:00 p.m.

On the morning of January 21, 1949, Maguire and Ormsby brought Robert Massey into the homicide interrogation room to confront Sewell. There, Massey related the admission by Sewell that he had gone to the tire shop on the night of December 20 to burglarize it and had struck Latham. Despite the claim, Sewell insisted that Massey was lying and continued to deny killing Latham.

On January 22, Maguire and Ormsby returned to the jail, where they conducted a third interview with Sewell, again in the presence of Massey. Unlike the previous interview, when he denied everything, this time Sewell said he wished to make a statement. He was walked to room 56 of Police Headquarters, where the homicide unit was housed. Today, room 56 is a retail shop within the restored Old Police Headquarters and is open to the public.

The confession was transcribed by Police Stenographer Helen Bohn, who served in the Homicide Unit from 1943 to 1962.

Sewell voluntarily admitted to going to the tire shop at about 8:00 or 8:30 on the night of December 20, 1945, intending to rob Latham. Sewell stated that he was not intoxicated. After entering the gate to the premises, Sewell said he picked up a piece of pipe then saw Latham checking up the day's receipts. Sewell said he waited for five or ten minutes until Latham walked out of the door of the office into the yard, at which time: "He walked out and I was standing right over there, and I just boom, let him have it. He was coming out of the door. I was standing like that. He made a step, and I just crowned him. He came out just like he is standing there, and I hit him on the head, and he fell on an angle like that, on his arm, and he didn't move, and I got kinda nervous."

Sewell said he searched Latham's pockets, pulled out his wallet, took approximately $100 from the desk and then ran out of the place. He said he returned to his hotel and told his wife he'd struck it rich. When she asked him where he had been, he said he "pulled a job" in Linda Vista.

Sewell said he and his wife left town shortly after being questioned by Detectives Wadman and Hughen. Sewell admitted he used some of the stolen money to pay his delinquent room rent of twenty dollars and to purchase two bus tickets to Los Angeles.

When detectives showed Sewell the pipe recovered at the crime scene, he responded, "I guess that's it." He then identified photographs taken of the premises and marked each one with his initials.

Afterward, Sewell read the confession typed up by Stenographer Bohn. After making corrections to punctuation and spelling, he initialed each page.

If detectives thought things would be smooth sailing with a confession, they quickly found themselves on the defensive when Sewell alleged he had been mistreated and that his statements were obtained under duress.

On January 25, 1949, the police department announced that Sergeants Maguire and Ormsby had arrested not only Robert Sewell but also Frank Flinn after the forty-one-year-old truck driver admitted to concealing Latham's wallet and a bottle of brandy that had been in the office.

The department said Flinn admitted that after he found Latham's body he picked up the discarded wallet and looked through it. Fearing his fingerprints would be found and he would be labeled a suspect, Flinn said he got rid of the wallet as well as a pint bottle of brandy in the office.

Chief of Police A.E. Jansen told the press, "Flinn's actions hindered the investigation of the murder as fingerprints could have been found on the shiny bottle and wallet." Jansen added that the police department had wasted resources sending out hundreds of photos of wallets similar to Latham's to police agencies across the United States in hopes of locating the valuable piece of evidence.

On January 25, detectives consulted the District Attorney's Office about charging Flinn with being an accessory to the crime. The DA declined to pursue charges, and later that day Flinn was released from custody after questioning and an agreement to cooperate with the ongoing investigation.

On March 1, 1949, Sewell was ordered by Judge A.F. Molina to answer to the charge of murder. His trial was scheduled for April 14.

On April 13, the local chapter of the National Association for the Advancement of Colored People (NAACP) held a rally for Sewell at the Logan Auditorium at Twenty-Eighth Street and Ocean View Boulevard. Gordon Stafford, the association's Civil Rights Committee chairman, told reporters, "The Association alleges that Sewell's confession to police was made under duress."

On April 15, Robert Sewell took the stand in his own defense and told the court that he had been severely beaten by Detective Hughen and another man he did not know. Sewell claimed he was struck in the stomach, ribs and kidneys, gouged in the eyes, kicked in the ribs and head and butted into the wall until he was "groggy."

Sewell said he confessed only because he believed "he was going to die one way or another." He added that he suffered from swelling of the eyes and a bad ear as aftereffects of the alleged beating; that when he arrived at the County Jail, after the statement had been taken, his eyes were still swollen.

The court then heard from a string of witnesses, among them an attorney who testified that he saw Sewell in the County Jail in the latter part of January or the first part of February and that at that time the defendant had some scratches on his cheeks. There was no evidence, however, to connect the scratches with a beating.

Another witness stated that he saw Sewell on January 22 in the city jail and that he had a bandage around his head. That allegation was countered by the jailer, who said that he had not noticed any bandage on Sewell's head but that he used a white handkerchief to hold down his hair while he slept.

Another defense witness testified that in the latter part of January he noticed the defendant's ear bleeding, but on cross-examination he couldn't remember which ear.

A doctor testified that he examined Sewell in the County Jail on March 10, 1949, and that he found a perforation of the defendant's left eardrum. On cross-examination, the doctor stated that he could not tell when the perforation occurred and conceded it could have occurred ten years earlier.

Robert Massey testified that when he saw Sewell the second time (shortly after the alleged beating), he looked the same as he always had. Massey further stated that the officers did not make any promises of reward or immunity, nor did they use any force on the defendant in his presence.

Detective Hughen declared that he made no threats against Sewell and did use force or violence on him. Hughen added that he was off work on

The testimony of Homicide Stenographer Helen Bohn was instrumental in refuting Robert Sewell's allegations of a forced confession. *Courtesy of San Diego Police Museum.*

January 21 and 22 and did not see Sewell on those days. SDPD payroll records corroborated the claim.

The Police Department then provided photos of Sewell taken on January 25, 1949, at the County Jail. The photos failed to show any indication of his eyes having been gouged and showed no marks on his face.

Lieutenant Morton Geer testified that he saw Sewell about 9:00 p.m. on January 22 and personally saw him read a statement and initial each page. Geer added that there were no marks, wounds, bruises or cuts on the defendant's face at that time and that his eyes were not swollen.

Detective Sergeant Maguire also testified to being present when Sewell confessed and that it was made freely and voluntarily. Maguire added that he never saw force or violence in any of the interviews when he was present.

Stenographer Helen Bohn testified that there were no bruises, cuts, wounds or injuries on Sewell and that he never complained about having suffered any such injuries. She said that, in her opinion, Sewell provided his confession freely and voluntarily. She added that she did not see any threats, promises or force or violence used against him.

Robert Massey told the jury that Sewell confessed to the crime four to six months after it occurred.

The eight-woman, four-man jury received the case on April 20, 1949. After a four-hour deliberation, they returned a unanimous guilty verdict of murder in the first degree, a crime punishable by execution in the gas chamber or life in prison. Sewell stood emotionless as the verdict was read. A woman later identified as his wife broke into tears and nearly collapsed in the spectator section of the courtroom.

On April 25, a defense motion for a new trial was denied by Judge William A. Glen. On May 2, 1949, Robert Sewell was sentenced to a life term in

CDC# V72100 Date: 05/11/2018

Until his death sentence was overturned, convicted wife slayer Scott Peterson resided in the same death row that once housed the man who killed his grandfather. *Courtesy of San Quentin.*

San Quentin prison. On February 2, 1950, Sewell's appeal was denied by the Fourth District Court of Appeals.

The sentence would turn out to be relatively short. On January 31, 1951, the *San Diego Union* reported that Robert Sewell died of pneumonia following a kidney ailment.

The aftermath of the Latham murder devastated the surviving family members. According to Jackie Latham, her mother, Helen, was so distraught that she could no longer care for them and that she and her siblings were placed in an orphanage.

Jackie made those comments to a court in 2004 as she testified in the penalty phase of her son, Scott Peterson, who had just been convicted of the murder of his wife, Laci, and their unborn son, Connor.

Jackie Latham Peterson passed away in 2013 at the age of seventy. Her son Scott is currently an inmate in the same prison that once housed the man who murdered his grandfather.

12

THE BLACK DAHLIA

JANUARY 15, 1947.

When young housewife Betty Bursinger discovered the mutilated body of a young, dark-haired female in a vacant lot in the Leimert Park district of Los Angeles, it launched one of the largest and most vexing murder cases in California history.

The dead woman had been surgically cut in half and drained of her blood. The body had been slashed and a leg tattoo cut off. A macabre smile had been deliberately carved into her face, and she was obscenely posed, as though the killer wanted to make one final, degrading statement. Even veteran policemen described the scene as remarkably cruel.

The crime would be indexed as case 295771, but the media would later immortalize it as the "Black Dahlia Murder."

Postmortem reports categorized the condition of the body as "surgically bisected," suggesting that someone with medical skills was related to her death.

Modern medical literature more specifically describes the mutilation as a hemicorporectomy, a radical surgery in which the body below the waist is amputated, transecting the lumbar spine and removing the legs, genitalia, urinary system, pelvic bones, anus and rectum. The procedure, which goes through the second and third lumbar vertebrae, is the only way a human body can be cut in half at the waist without sawing through bone.

Because she was nude, the only hope the Los Angeles Police Department had to identify the victim, classified as Jane Doe number one, was through fingerprints. After an exhaustive search through the repository of inked print cards in the LAPD Identification Bureau, they turned to the Federal Bureau of Investigation for assistance.

At that time, absent U.S. mail or a special courier, the LAPD had no way to get the prints to FBI Headquarters in Washington, D.C. The *Los Angeles Examiner* allowed the LAPD to use a mimeograph machine to transmit her prints to FBI Headquarters, marking first time in police history fingerprints were electronically transmitted.

The FBI connected the prints to nineteen-year-old Elizabeth Short, a native of Medford, Massachusetts. The high school dropout had been arrested in 1944 for underage

Elizabeth Short always sought fame. Ironically, it was her brutal murder that brought the worldwide attention she could never attain while she was alive. *Courtesy Los Angeles Police Department.*

drinking. The LAPD learned that Short, who bore a strong resemblance to movie star Deanna Durbin, began calling herself the "Black Dahlia" to draw attention to her penchant for always wearing black.

Captain Jack Donohue was the ranking officer for the LAPD. Armed with a name, his detectives began looking into how she turned up in a vacant lot seven miles southwest of downtown Los Angeles.

Within days, the Black Dahlia Murder dominated newspaper and shock-magazine headlines across most of the United States.

Captain Donohue's investigators learned that Elizabeth was born in Medford and moved to the West Coast in 1943, originally to live with her father, Cleo, in Oakland. Cleo Short had abandoned his wife and five daughters in the 1930s by staging his own death. Years later, he wrote a letter to the family. On learning that her father was alive, Elizabeth made plans to travel west to live with him.

When police contacted Cleo about the death of his daughter, he told them he "wanted nothing to do with this."

After speaking to Cleo, detectives traced her movements south to Camp Cook, a World War II military base just north of Santa Barbara, where she landed a job at the Post Exchange. While at the camp, she won a beauty contest as the "Camp Cutie."

It was there that Elizabeth was arrested for underage drinking. She was booked and photographed. She drifted from Camp Cook to Los Angeles and then Florida. She wound up back on the West Coast at the end of the war.

Steve Hodel, a retired Los Angeles Police detective, has extensively researched the Black Dahlia case and has even gone so far as to declare his father, Dr. George Hodel, MD, her killer.

In a January 22, 2022 interview with KFI News, Steve Hodel described Elizabeth as "a lost soul. She was drifting, looking for love. After her murder, a number of hack writers tried to paint her as an alcoholic, prostitute and a loser. She was none of those things. She was just a 22-year-old girl looking to fall in love."

San Diego PD Chief of Detectives Michael E. Donnelly received the formal request for assistance on January 16, 1947. He detailed Detective Lieutenant Ed Deickmann to oversee the investigation. Detectives Thomas Stotler, Gerald LaFond, Russel Ormsby and George Orr were to assist.

Through tips and investigation, the team determined that Elizabeth had arrived in San Diego via bus in early December 1946. Broke and homeless, Elizabeth found refuge in the all-night Aztec movie theater at Fifth & G Streets downtown. There, she met twenty-five-year-old ticket girl Dorothy French.

After discovering Elizabeth sleeping in the seats, Dorothy invited her to stay with her family at their modest Pacific Beach home at 2750 Camino Pradera in the Bayview Terraces housing development—a racially integrated neighborhood of locally designed and hastily constructed duplexes built to house San Diego's exploding World War II population.

Life there was very basic. Wartime residents described it as a tidy utopia where the landlords provided free paint and grass seed and fostered a terrific sense of camaraderie among the renters, mostly defense-industry workers. Later, the project became a low-income housing tract often for the down and out who couldn't afford to live anywhere else.

Lieutenant Dieckmann met with the French family at their home on the evening of January 16, 1947.

The matriarch, Elvera "Vera" French, told Dieckmann that Elizabeth presented herself as the widow of a World War II pilot killed in combat. Elizabeth also claimed that the couple had a child but that the baby died.

Vera described Elizabeth as shy and mysterious and more interested in dating men than getting a job. Vera told Lieutenant Dieckmann she worried about allowing a young woman to live on her couch and the effect it had on her ten-year-old son.

An artist's rendering based on newspaper clippings and blueprints provide a glimpse of life in the post–World War II public housing block on the eastern edge of Pacific Beach. *Courtesy of Viet Do.*

Dorothy said that during her stay Elizabeth seemed constantly in fear and was even frightened anytime someone came to the door. Vera recounted an incident in which two men and a woman drove up to the house and knocked on the door "in the late hour." When no one answered, the trio ran back to the car, then drove off. Vera said that when she asked Elizabeth about it, she seemed very frightened and reluctant to talk.

According to the French family members, Elizabeth spent time at Sheldon's Café, located at what was then part of Pacific Highway. (The site was demolished years ago and would now be located in the 4700 block of Mission Bay Drive.)

According to the *San Diego Union*, Vera provided Lieutenant Dieckmann with a black scarf and a dark, crown-top model hat that Elizabeth had left behind as "a gift from the Black Dahlia wardrobe."

Vera concluded the interview by stating that the last time she saw Elizabeth was on January 8, 1947, when she left with a slender, well-mannered, well-dressed man, approximately six feet tall with a fair completion and freckles. Vera said she believed the man was named either "Bob" or "Red."

As their boss met with the French family, Detectives Ormsby and LaFond visited Western Union for communications sent to Elizabeth. One item of interest was a January 8, 1947 telegram from Los Angeles that read, "Wait and I'll be down for you." It was signed "Red."

Acting on a tip that Red could be an ex–Marine Corps pilot from Huntington Beach, Ormsby and LaFond spent the day checking airports and hotels for anyone matching the description of Red. They came up empty. The LAPD later identified one possible "Red" as Robert Manley, a married traveling salesman who lived in Los Angeles.

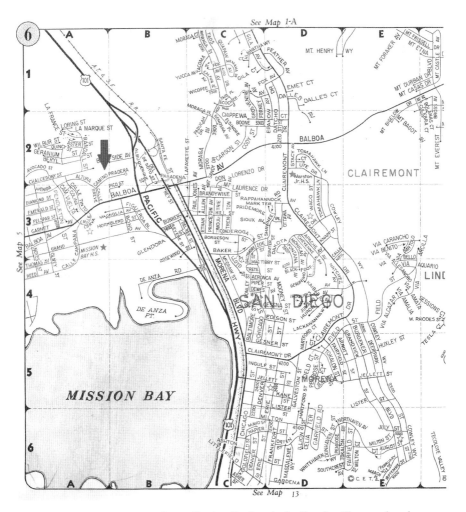

A 1953 Thomas Brother map shows Camino Pradera in the Bayview Terraces housing development. The entire neighborhood, even the streets, were razed in 1959 to make way for more modern housing. *Courtesy of San Diego Police Museum.*

More investigative follow-up revealed that while the French family supported her, Elizabeth sent a letter to her mother, Phebe, stating that she was living with a girlfriend and was employed at the San Diego Naval Hospital. In reality, it was Vera who worked at the Naval Hospital. There is no record of Elizabeth ever being employed there.

Detectives also learned that while residing with the French family, Elizabeth was soliciting friends for money and a place to live.

Detectives visited Sheldon's and spoke with waitresses Jadell Grey and Adeleine McSwain. Both remembered Elizabeth and went so far as to say she had a favorite chair at the diner. Both women said the last time they saw her was on the fourteenth, accompanied by a "vain," well-dressed ginger who was constantly looking at himself in a mirror. When shown a photo of Red Manley, both women insisted that he was not the mysterious redhead.

Detectives next interviewed R.H. Goldsmith, who worked at a service station next to Sheldon's. Goldsmith told detectives he saw Elizabeth on January 14 at a nearby bus stop. Goldsmith said he remembered her because of her stunning looks and cheery demeanor.

Dieckmann's men weren't so sure. According to the Los Angeles County Coroner, Elizabeth had been dead at least ten hours when she was found. Considering that a drive from San Diego to Los Angeles would have been 120 miles along a two-lane coastal highway with traffic lights, the timeline didn't fit.

They continued to scour the city for leads. The only other item of interest was the irony of where Elizabeth spent her last night in San Diego: the Aztec Theatre, watching the Raymond Chandler feature *The Blue Dahlia*. In that movie, one of the characters, Helen, is the victim of a homicide.

At 2:15 a.m. on January 29, 1947, Emily Williams of 3457 Victory Street walked into San Diego Police Headquarters and spoke to the front desk officer: "I want to confess. The Black Dahlia stole my man so I killed her and cut her up."

Lieutenant Dieckmann was summoned from home to interrogate the twenty-four-year-old blond waitress. The lengthy interview that ensued ended with Dieckmann declaring it a hoax. Williams's attempt to get her name in the newspapers cost her thirty days in jail.

As one might expect, Manley was a prime suspect in the case. He told Los Angeles Police detectives that he picked up Elizabeth on January 8, 1947, from Camino Pradera and they spent that afternoon and evening watching movies; then they went dancing and drinking. They ended the night in a Pacific Beach motel. Manley said Elizabeth had too much to drink, so one of them slept on the bed while the other slept on a chair. They left for Los Angeles the next day.

Manley said he last saw Elizabeth when he dropped her off at the swanky Biltmore Hotel in downtown Los Angeles. It marked the last known time anyone saw her alive.

Poster for the movie *The Blue Dahlia*. *Wikipedia*.

Multiple LAPD interrogations and a polygraph eventually cleared Manley as a suspect. He died on January 9, 1986, exactly thirty-nine years to the day he and the Black Dahlia had parted ways.

In a creepy coincidence, just days after Elizabeth was found, another Los Angeles woman was brutally murdered. Her nude, mutilated body was strewn in a vacant field and "B.D." was drawn across her stomach with lipstick. The victim's last name was French—no relation to the family Elizabeth had stayed with while in San Diego.

Appendix
THE CHARACTERS

JASPER L. "JACK" BERG served the SDPD from 1915 until his retirement as Chief of Detectives on October 14, 1936. He was fifty-three years old and in failing health when, on September 11, 1942, he took his own life in the garage of his home at 4715 Thirteenth Street.

HELEN BOHN worked her entire eighteen-year career in the Homicide Bureau as a stenographer. She left the department in 1961 when she married Detective Sergeant Cody Isbell. The pair retired to the Midwest, where she passed away on October 2, 1986.

DR. PAUL BRUST, MD, was the primary police surgeon and the only full-time medical doctor assigned to the San Diego Police Emergency Hospital. During his twenty-year career with the San Diego Police Department, he played a part in some of the department's most high-profile, violent cases. He retired on June 30, 1946. In 1949, Dr. Brust told the *San Diego Union* that he missed his time in the police department. He passed away on December 26, 1959.

RICHARD W. CHADWICK SR. was the father of Florence Chadwick, the first woman to swim the English Channel. Richard began his police career in 1910 and served until 1931, when he retired as a Detective Sergeant. He was the first of a number of Chadwicks to serve the San Diego Police Department. Richard passed away on November 3, 1951.

FRED H. CHRISTENSEN served the SDPD from 1940 to 1960. He passed away on February 10, 1963. His son, Officer Frank Christensen, also served a full police career in San Diego.

EDWARD F. COOPER served as San Diego County Sheriff from 1929 to 1935. According to that department's website, Sheriff Cooper is remembered most for forming the county's first industrial road camp and the creation of a Juvenile Delinquency Division with the Sheriff's Department. He died on November 26, 1962.

LAMBERTON "BERT" COOPER served the SDPD from 1927 until an on-duty injury ended his career in 1930. He died on April 24, 1959.

ROBERT CREASON served the San Diego Police Department from 1946 to 1955, when his experience and expertise with homicide investigations pushed him to become a deputy coroner for San Diego County. He died on September 16, 2018.

EDWARD A. DIECKMANN SR. was hired at the rank of detective in May 1931 and never wore a police uniform during his twenty-three-year police career. When he retired as the Homicide Bureau Lieutenant in 1954, he was generally regarded as one of the nation's preeminent experts on murder investigations. He died on November 25, 1973.

JOSEPH V. DORAN served the SDPD from 1916 to 1945. During his two-year tenure as Chief of Police (1927–29), he made reorganizing the police department and getting rid of policewomen among his top priorities. He retired as a Captain on September 25, 1945, and passed away on May 14, 1950.

DAVID GERSHON came to the SDPD in 1912 after working as Chief of Detectives for the Oklahoma City Police Department. He left SDPD in 1915. After stints in federal law enforcement and the private sector, he became a deputy coroner in 1931. He suffered a fatal heart attack on October 5, 1939.

ERNEST HANCE served from 1923 to 1944. A veteran of both world wars, he passed away on February 15, 1973.

PAUL J. HAYES was the first of three generations of his family to serve the SDPD. He began his law enforcement career as a patrolman on January 23, 1911. He became a member of the bureau when he was appointed as an Inspector of lost and stolen property on July 30, 1913. He retired on June 15, 1931, as the Chief of Detectives. He died on March 10, 1947.

EDWARD HERTING JR. was the former partner of disgraced former policeman Gerhard Cordes. He served a twenty-year career (1932–52). In 1938, he made local news when he and another officer scaled down a two-hundred-foot cliff and then dove into the ocean to save the life of a person in distress. Officer Herting passed away in March 1973.

ARTHUR HILL served as Chief from 1929 to 1931 before City Hall politics led to him voluntarily demoting to the rank of Captain. He retired after a twenty-two-year career in 1931. He passed away on April 26, 1960. His wife, Ida Griffin, was one of the first San Diego Police Matrons, serving from 1912 to 1929.

CHARLES HUGHEN ended his twenty-year career as a lieutenant overseeing the Homicide Unit. He passed away on November 4, 1990.

JOHN A. KANE was a U.S. Navy veteran who saw combat in both world wars. During his SDPD tenure, Kane balanced his career between the uniformed patrol division and the bureau. He served the SDPD from June 4, 1923, until he left to serve in World War II in 1943. He passed away on March 27, 1977.

HARRY J. KELLY served a twenty-eight-year SDPD career, most of it in the Detective Bureau, where he served at every rank. Kelly also served as the interim Chief of Police for ninety days in 1939. He retired in 1943 and passed away on February 4, 1955.

GERALD LAFOND began his twenty-five-year SDPD career on August 1, 1941. He retired as a Lieutenant in charge of forgery and auto theft.

FRED E. "JERRY" LIGHTNER served the San Diego Police Department from 1923 until his untimely death from pneumonia on September 21, 1937. In his eulogy, Chief George Sears described Lightner as "one of the most capable officers we have ever had."

JOSEPH LOPEZ, a San Diego native, was born in an Old Town adobe in 1877. During his career (1910–36), he never had an identified suspect escape him. He died on December 13, 1939, after a long illness.

LEO MAGONE served the San Diego Police Department from 1928 to 1948 and was the first officer to be assigned to a two-way radio patrol car. He died on August 24, 1971.

ANTHONY J. MAGUIRE served the San Diego Police Department from 1935 to 1955. At his retirement at the rank of Detective Sergeant, Maguire recounted the Latham murder case as the most challenging of his career. He died in October 1973.

BLAKE MASON served the San Diego County Sheriff's Department from 1931 to 1954, when he retired at the rank of captain. During his career, he partnered with his SDPD counterparts in some of the region's most difficult crime cases. A true legend in law enforcement, he passed away on November 3, 1967, after undergoing heart surgery.

NATHANIEL MCHORNEY was the last Chief of the East San Diego Police Department. He joined the SDPD when the City of East San Diego ceased to exist in January 1924. With an expertise in murder investigation, he served as a detective until his retirement in 1940. He died on June 5, 1956.

JUDSON MEADE served from 1916 to 1936 and was one of the last officers to patrol the city exclusively on a bicycle. He died on February 25, 1964.

LLOYD MIERS served in the Identification and Records Bureau, then later at the upstart crime lab, from 1928 to 1948. He passed away on November 12, 1954.

ORAN MUIR was one of San Diego's most experienced prosecutors. He died on October 7, 1935, of a ruptured blood vessel in his modest South Park bungalow. He had been sick for more than a year after falling ill during closing arguments of the Gerhard Cordes murder trial.

OLGA NELSON was forced to resign after shooting an attacker in Balboa Park and a 1928 purge of policewomen within the ranks of the police department. She passed away on December 17, 1965, in Escondido, California

ROBERT NEWSOM served the San Diego Police Department from 1916 until his on-duty death on February 11, 1936. During his career, he served at all ranks, including a short time as Chief of Police.

RUSSELL ORMSBY served the SDPD from 1941 to 1962, when he retired as a Detective Sergeant. In the early 1950s, both he and Anthony Maguire were featured on the true crime radio show *Dragnet* when the fictitious LAPD Sergeant Joe Friday had cases that wound up in San Diego. He died in December 1979.

GEORGE ORR served from 1941 until his retirement as a Detective Sergeant in 1968. He died on December 21, 1993.

CHARLES PADGETT was a veteran of both world wars and served a nineteen-year career. He was still an active-duty detective when he succumbed to a long-term illness on January 5, 1948.

HARRY RAYMOND served less than four months as SDPD Chief before returning to Los Angeles to work as a private investigator. In 1938, he was investigating graft at Los Angeles City Hall when a bomb exploded in his car. He somehow survived, and his testimony before the Grand Jury brought down the Mayor, the Chief of Police and ten members of the LAPD. His last contact with the SDPD was in 1957, when he was arrested on a charge of being drunk in public. He died on April 1, 1957.

HAROLD REAMA was a veteran of both world wars and served the SDPD from 1915 until 1935. After World War II, he returned to public service when he became the first Chief of the Imperial Beach Police Department, a now-defunct agency. Reama also served as a member of the Imperial Beach City Council and as Vice-Mayor. He died on August 11, 1962.

CLARENCE RENNER served his entire career (1926–46) as a motorcycle officer. In the 1960s, he provided SDPD's historian, Sergeant Edward W.

Kenney, numerous artifacts and career highlights that now reside in the San Diego Police Museum. He died on June 4, 1986.

GEORGE SEARS spent most of his SDPD career in the Detective Bureau. In the early 1930s, Sears was a lieutenant, and his officers spent the majority of their time enforcing liquor laws. Known as the "Dry Squad," the five-officer team led raids on speakeasies and distilleries around the city. Sears was appointed Chief of Police in 1934 and served until his retirement on June 27, 1939. He died on March 28, 1974.

OLEN SIMMONS served the San Diego Police Department from 1930 to 1944, when he left the department at the rank of Lieutenant to open a café. He passed away on November 9, 1948.

THOMAS "ED" STOTLER began his law enforcement career as a police lifeguard in 1928. He became a sworn police officer in April 1934. Stotler retired in January 1968. He died on September 28, 1986.

FRANK E. TOOMEY, MD, came to San Diego in 1926 after graduating from Creighton Medical School. Originally in private practice, he joined the Medical Examiner's Office in 1931. He ended his twenty-six-year career in 1957 as the Chief Autopsy Surgeon for the county of San Diego. He died on June 7, 1960.

ELMER WADMAN served SDPD from 1940 to 1960. With a strong interest in forensics, he was involved with some of San Diego's most high-profile cases of the day. He ended his twenty-year career as a lieutenant in charge of the police crime lab. He passed away on August 30, 1995.

PAUL WALK served the San Diego Police Department from 1938 to 1956. He passed away on July 12, 1986.

THOMAS A. WHELAN was elected in 1931 as San Diego County's top prosecutor. At the age of twenty-eight, he was the youngest person elected to the office. He served until 1938, when he left for private practice. He returned to office in 1941 but left again in 1946 when he chose to not run for reelection. His son Thomas John Whelan is a Senior U.S. District Judge of the U.S. District Court for the Southern District of California.

RENA WRIGHT was forced to resign when the police department purged the ranks of policewomen in 1928. She passed away on November 19, 1958, in Lemon Grove, California.

BIBLIOGRAPHY

1. A Long, Painful Demise

San Diego Evening Tribune.
San Diego Police Department case files. San Diego Police Museum. San Diego, California.
San Diego Police Museum archives. San Diego, California.
San Diego Union.
Webster family archives.

2. Ambush in the Park

Charles Harris inquest transcripts.
Harris family artifacts.
San Diego Evening Tribune.
San Diego Police Department case files. San Diego Police Museum. San Diego, California.
San Diego Police Museum archives. San Diego, California.
San Diego Union.

3. Innocence Stolen

Dieckmann, Ed. Career memoirs. San Diego Police Museum archives. San Diego, California.

San Diego County Coroner. Official inquest transcripts.

San Diego Evening Tribune.

San Diego Police Department case files. San Diego Police Museum. San Diego, California.

San Diego Police Museum archives. San Diego, California.

San Diego Sun.

San Diego Union.

4. Louise Teuber

San Diego County Coroner. Official inquest transcripts.

San Diego Evening Tribune.

San Diego Police Museum archives. San Diego, California.

San Diego Union.

5. Diamond Dolly

Dieckmann, Ed. Career memoirs. San Diego Police Museum archives. San Diego, California.

San Diego County Coroner. Official inquest transcripts.

San Diego Evening Tribune.

San Diego Police Department case files. San Diego Police Museum. San Diego, California.

San Diego Police Museum archives. San Diego, California.

San Diego Union.

6. The Indian Village Murderer

San Diego County Coroner. Official inquest transcripts.

San Diego Evening Tribune.

San Diego Police Department case files. San Diego Police Museum. San Diego, California.

San Diego Police Museum archives. San Diego, California.
San Diego Union.

7. A Most Unlikely Suspect

Dieckmann, Ed. Career memoirs. San Diego Police Museum archives. San
    Diego, California.
San Diego County Coroner. Official inquest transcripts.
San Diego Evening Tribune.
San Diego Police Department case files. San Diego Police Museum. San
    Diego, California.
San Diego Police Museum archives. San Diego, California.
San Diego Union.

8. The Coldest Case

Las Vegas Review Journal.
Nathaniel McHorney career memoirs.
San Diego Evening Tribune.
San Diego Police Department case files. San Diego Police Museum. San
    Diego, California.
San Diego Police Museum archives. San Diego, California.
San Diego Union.

9. Celia Cota

Dieckmann, Ed. Career memoirs. San Diego Police Museum archives. San
    Diego, California.
San Diego County Coroner. Official inquest transcripts.
San Diego Evening Tribune.
San Diego Police Department case files. San Diego Police Museum. San
    Diego, California.
San Diego Police Museum archives. San Diego, California.
San Diego Union.
San Francisco Examiner.

10. A Guilty Conscience

Dieckmann, Ed. Career memoirs. San Diego Police Museum archives. San Diego, California.
San Diego County Coroner. Official inquest transcripts.
San Diego Police Department case files. San Diego Police Museum. San Diego, California.
San Diego Police Museum archives. San Diego, California.
Waters, Mark. *Startling Detective* (September 1955).

11. A Homicidal Irony

Dieckmann, Ed. Career memoirs. San Diego Police Museum archives. San Diego, California.
San Diego Evening Tribune.
San Diego Police Department case files. San Diego Police Museum. San Diego, California.
San Diego Police Museum archives. San Diego, California.
San Diego Union.

12. The Black Dahlia

Dieckmann, Ed. Career memoirs. San Diego Police Museum archives. San Diego, California.
Ferrara, Bernard E. "Hemicorporectomy: A Collective Review." *Journal of Surgical Oncology* (December 1990).
Hodel, Steve. *Black Dahlia Avenger: The True Story.* New York: HarperCollins, 2006.
Los Angeles Examiner.
San Diego Evening Tribune.
San Diego Police Department case files. San Diego Police Museum. San Diego, California.
San Diego Police Museum archives. San Diego, California.
San Diego Union.

ABOUT THE AUTHOR

T he son of a police chief and the grandson of a fire chief, Steve Willard has resided in San Diego since 1977. After joining the San Diego Police Department in 1985, he has worked patrol, crime prevention, investigations, traffic and administration. He became a charter member of the San Diego Police Museum in 1997 and currently serves as the organization's vice-president.

A court-certified expert in crime scene investigation and domestic violence, Willard delivers a unique insider prospective to true crime writing. In addition to authoring four books on the San Diego Police Department, he serves as a lecturer on department history and has more than two decades of experience as contributing columnist to several law enforcement publications.

Visit us at
www.historypress.com